BEAD WEAVING
C L A S S I C S

by TAKAKO SAKO

TRANSLATED FROM JAPANESE by CONNIE PRENER

edited by Jules & Kaethe Kliot

LACIS PUBLICATIONS

Material in this book is from the original Japanese language work by Takako Sako
CLASSICAL BEAD WEAVING (translated) ISBN 4-14-031050-2
published by NHK Publishing (Japan Broadcast Publishing Co., Ltd)
Tokyo, Japan in 1990
©1990 Takako Sako

English translation: Connie Prener
Cover design and layout: Goji Morofuji
Photography: Masayuki Tsutsui
Stylist: Yoko Watanabe
Illustrations: Chikami Okuda, Chiaki Sakagawa, Kiyoshi Suzuki, Yukiyo Betchaku
Photo props: Kiya Gallery, Kensington, Shinagawa Rekishikan, Y Chic

English language edition published by

LACIS PUBLICATIONS
3163 Adeline Street
Berkeley, CA 94703

ISBN 1-891656-20-1
Printed in China

PUBLISHER'S NOTES

Basic loom and finishing techniques, which were part of the original text and which are included in the authors prior translated works have been omitted from this edition.

The instructions presented in this book assume some general knowledge of bead weaving.

Instructions for loom set up will depend on specific loom used and reference should be made to manufacturer's instructions.

Specific instructions offered in this book are a translation from the Japanese as originally offered by the author with minor editing as required for clarity.

Reference should be made to the authors prior translated publications
BEAD WEAVING: ACCESSORIES by Takako Sako &
BEAD WEAVING: ELEGANCE by Takako Sako
published by LACIS PUBLICATIONS

All dimensions are given in metric units, unchanged from the original Japanese language editions. To convert millimeters to inches, multiply by .0394. For example 20mm equals .79 inches.

Specific beads and hardware items shown in this book might not be readily available. Inquiries can be made to publisher for current sources of supplies and alternatives.

A wide, 11" bead weaving loom, illustrated on page 128, specifically designed for two-needle bead weaving is available from this publisher.

Publishers comments within text are noted within *[...]*

PROFILE OF AUTHOR, TAKAKO SAKO

Takako Sako was born in Hiroshima.

Captivated by some antique beadwork she discovered in 1973 during a sojourn in New York City, she began studying the craft with Dr. Esthel Popham at Columbia University. Soon she was creating her own designs.

Currently, she teaches and is engaged in research on bead weaving techniques, producing innovative contemporary designs for the current age.

Ms. Sako teaches bead weaving in her Creative Bead Weaving class in the adult education school in Japan.

INTRODUCTION

I have treasured beads ever since I was a child.
When I was in junior high school, a bead factory opened up near my home
and I spent many happy hours with the beautiful beads I bought there -
I used them in my crocheting and embroidery projects, and
to decorate pictures I had drawn.

During a visit to someone's home 17 years ago, when I was living in
New York, I was shown some bead woven handbags and purses. They
were quite old. Some of the threads were broken, and the color
of the beads had faded over the years. But the patterns and
colors evoked an elegance that totally fascinated me.

It was then that my involvement with beads deepened irrevocably so.
My first bead weaving venture, for which I made my own loom by driving
nails into a block of wood, began soon after that.

In those days I had great difficulty getting a needle
through the holes in the beads. Today, fortunately, a wide
variety of glass beads made especially for weaving is available,
ranging in color from gold to transparent, and providing endless
possibilities for color combinations and effects. Now I have
the luxury of using beads as artists use their paints, creating
precisely the patterns and color combinations that I like.

One of the more enjoyable aspects of bead weaving for me
is the process of weaving the beads, one by one, following the
pattern I have drawn. The satisfaction I derive from completing
a project after I have spent many hours weaving,
row by row, is even greater.

In this book, I have expanded on basic designs for bags and purses,
adding innovative finishing touches such as fringe. I sincerely hope that
it will inspire readers to let their imaginations run free, and
experience the joy of creating something very special.

Finally, I wish to convey my heartfelt thanks to the staff of
NHK Publishing Co., Masayuki Tsutsui for his beautiful photography,
to designer Goji Morofuji, editor Mamiko Shibasaki, and the many
instructors who assisted me in the preparation of this book.

Takako Sako
September 1990

TABLE OF CONTENTS

SHOULDER BAG WITH
TRIANGLE MOTIF
Instructions on Page 82

BROOCH
Instructions on Page 81

EARRINGS
Instructions on Page 81

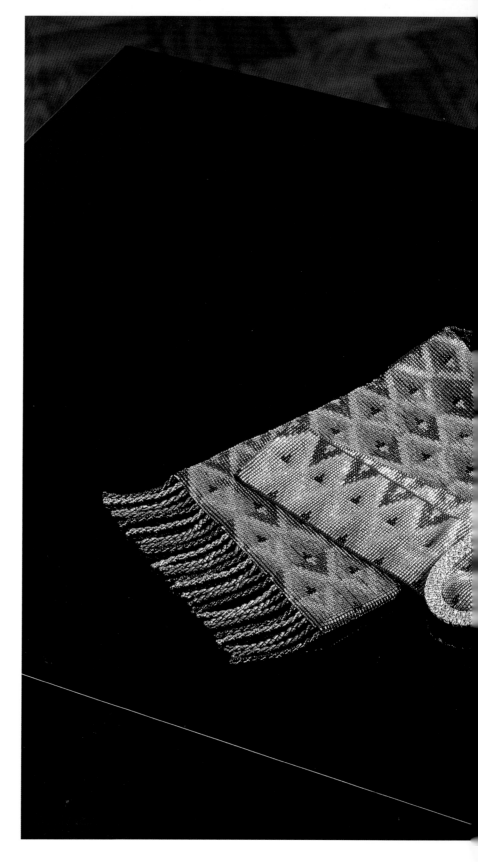

BAG WITH DIAMOND MOTIF
Instructions on Page 84

BELT
Instructions on Page 84

BAG WITH RIPPLE MOTIF
Instructions on Page 86

PURSE WITH GIRL AND FLOWERS
Instructions on Page 91

ACCESSORIES WITH FLOWER MOTIFS

PENDANT
Instructions on Page 88

BROOCH
Instructions on Page 88

EARRINGS
Instructions on Page 90

BRACELET
Instructions on Page 91

SILVER PURSE WITH FRINGE
Instructions on Page 76

SILVER CHOKER
Instructions on Page 51

ALPHABET BAG
Instructions on Page 60

BOUQUET BROOCH
Instructions on Page 48

HAT BROOCH
Instructions on Page 94

PARASOL BROOCH
Instructions on Page 95

BAG WITH ROSES
Instructions on Page 100

LIPSTICK HOLDER
Instructions on Page 98

BELT
Instructions on Page 98

PURSE WITH ROSES
Instructions on Page 106

PURSE WITH TINY ROSES
Instructions on Page 68

GOLD BAG WITH ROSES
Instructions on Page 102

GOLD CORSAGE
Instructions on Page 103

DIAMOND NECKLACE
Instructions on Page 50

BAG WITH ARABESQUE MOTIF
Instructions on Page 64

BAG WITH
EGYPTIAN MOTIF
Instructions on Page 72

TWO BROOCHES
WITH EGYPTIAN
MOTIFS
Instructions on Page 108

BAG WITH ASIAN MOTIFS
Instructions on Page 110

ROSE CORSAGE
Instructions on Page 56

PERFUME VIAL HOLDER
Instructions on Page 114

PAISLEY POCHETTE
Instructions on Page 112

PURSE INSPIRED BY
THE *TSUJIGAHANA*
(ILLUSIONARY) DYEING
STYLE
Instructions on Page 115

PURSE WITH
JAPANESE-STYLE
FLOWER PATTERN
Instructions on Page 118

SMALL ENVELOPE
PURSE
Instructions on Page 122

BAG WITH TORTOISE-
SHELL PATTERN
Instructions on Page 120

Tapestry with
Native American motif
Instructions on Page 52

MATERIALS & TECHNIQUES

[Basic loom and finishing techniques, which were part of the original text and which are included in the authors prior translated works have been omitted from this edition.

The instructions presented in this book assume some general knowledge of bead weaving.

Instructions for loom set up will depend on specific loom used and reference should be made to manufacturer's instructions.

Specific instructions offered in this book are a translation from the Japanese as originally offered by the author with minor editing as required for clarity.

Reference should also be made to page 126 where the 2-needle bead-weaving technique, preferred by this publisher, is described.]

BEADS

Select glass beads with a metallic luster. They are, approximately 1 mm long x 1.2 mm in diameter with large holes through which a needle will pass easily. Your finished work will have a delicate feel, and the metallic accents in the beads will give it an antique look. The beads come in two shapes, cut and cylindrical and can have a shinny or matte finish. *[Readily available Size 11 pre-strung seed beads are suggested for the projects in this book.]*

THREAD

No. 60 polyester thread is normally used for both weft and warp. Gray thread is used for most projects, but other colors of thread can also produce interesting, delightful results, depending on the overall color scheme. For instance, white thread works well with bright-colored, transparent beads. *[Bonded Nylon, which is resistant to splitting, in size B (fine) or C (medium) is an appropriate substitute.]*

Place beads in small boxes, one for each color. When only a few beads remain in a box, tilt it to one side so that they congregate in one corner and can be picked up easily.

[Placing double sticky tape on small cards is another way of handling beads. Beads poured on the tape will stay in place making individual beads easy to pick up with your needle. If working with pre-strung beads, the beads can be easily transferred to your beading needle by simply running the needle through the beads while keeping the strand taut.]

Joining Woven Pieces

There are two ways to join woven pieces.

Method "A" is used when there are no warp threads extending from the edges, for instance, when the pieces are large, or when one or the other (or both) are to be joined at a location other than an edge.

Method B is used when there are warp threads extending from both pieces, for instance, when you are joining the ends of a necklace or the edges of a purse woven horizontally (see photographs on Pages 20 and 22).

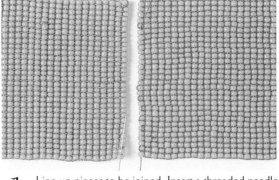

1   Line up pieces to be joined. Insert a threaded needle into the last row of one of the pieces (not at the very top), pass it through the beads in that row, and bring it out at the bottom of the row. Pick up two beads at the bottom of the other piece.

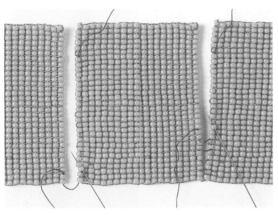

2   Pick up the third and fourth beads on the first row of the piece in which you first inserted the needle. Alternate between pieces, picking up two beads at a time, until you have reached the top.

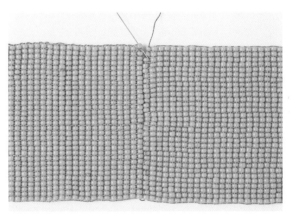

3   Pick up one bead from the top of each piece.

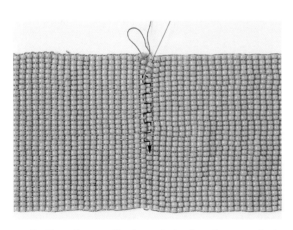

4   Pass the needle through the beads not picked up previously, two at a time, alternating between pieces and moving downward.

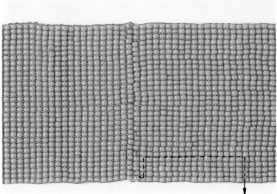

5   Hide thread by passing the needle through beads to one side.

Method "B"

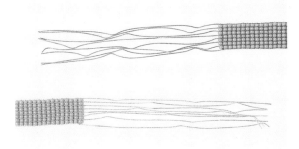

1   Cut warp threads on both pieces to a length of 15 cm.

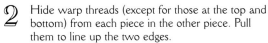

2   Hide warp threads (except for those at the top and bottom) from each piece in the other piece. Pull them to line up the two edges.

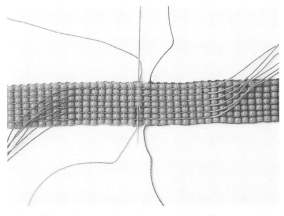

3   Thread a needle with one of the four remaining warp threads. Pass it through the beads at the edge of the other piece and bring it out in the middle of the row.

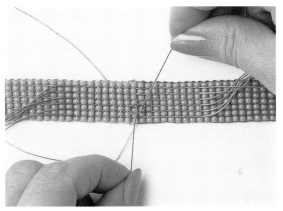

4   Repeat the process with the other warp thread on the same piece. Tie threads together at the center of the row.

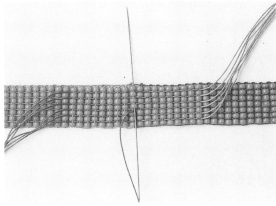

5   Pass the ends of the threads through several beads and cut.

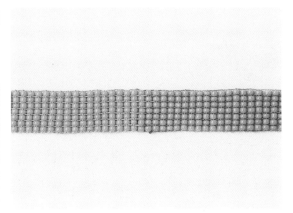

6   Repeat the process again with the two warp threads on the other piece.

FRINGE & EDGING

The length of fringe strands, the distance between them, and the number of beads in a picot vary with each design. Looped fringe (shown on Page 45) can be left long or made into edging, as shown in the photographs that follow.

A. STRAIGHT FRINGE

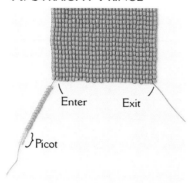

1 Insert needle into the first row of beads from the right side. Bring it out on the left side. Thread the required number of beads on needle.

2 After stringing the beads for the picot, pass the needle back through the other beads on the strand of fringe.

B. CRISS-CROSS FRINGE

1 Begin as you would to make straight fringe. Skipping two beads, insert needle into fourth bead from left, from the right, forming a circle.

2 String the beads for the second strand. Wind second strand around the beads in the first strand three times, from the right.

C. TWISTED FRINGE

1 Begin as you would to make straight fringe. String the beads for the first strand. Rotate strand several times to the right.

2 Pass needle through two beads to the right and pull thread, forming a strand of twisted fringe.

3 When you reach the right edge, tie and hide threads.

 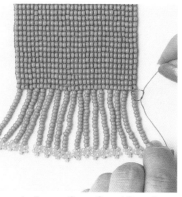 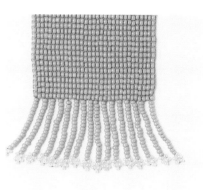

3 Pass the needle through two beads (more or less, depending on the space desired between the strands) to the right on the first row and pull thread.

4 Repeat Steps 2 and 3 until you reach the right side. Tie beginning and end of thread together in a square knot.

5 Hide threads.

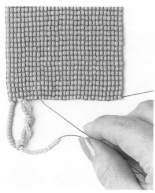 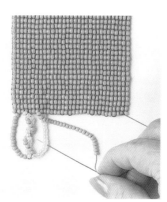 

3 Pick up the third bead to the right of the previous strand and pull thread.

4 Repeat Steps 2 and 3.

5 When you reach the right edge, pass needle through the last bead. Tie and hide threads.

D. LOOPED FRINGE

  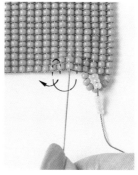 

1 Starting at the right edge, string beads for the first strand. Skip two rows. From the bottom, pass needle through two beads in the fourth row.

2 Pass needle through two beads on the next row to the right, bringing it out at the bottom edge.

3 String beads for the next strand of fringe. Skip one row and pass needle through two beads.

4 Repeat Steps 1-3.

45

E. NETTED FRINGE

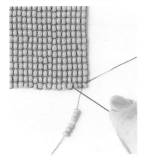

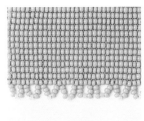

1 Pass a needle through the first bead at the bottom right edge. String the beads for the first mesh.

2 Skipping two beads, pick up the next bead at the edge. String the beads for the next mesh and, again skipping two beads, pick up the next bead.

3 Repeat Step 2 until you have reached the left side and completed the first row of netting.

4 Pass needle through first three beads of first mesh at left side of first row of netting. Make strand of straight fringe. Pass needle through bead at center of first mesh in first row. String beads for next mesh.

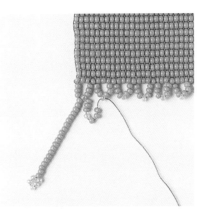

5 Pass the needle through the bead at the center of the next mesh on the first row. Pull thread.

6 Repeat Step 5. When second row is completed, make a strand of straight fringe at right edge. Pass needle through the bead at center of first row and beads at right side of first mesh in second row, bringing it out in center of that mesh.

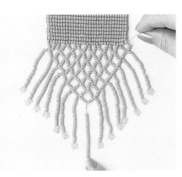

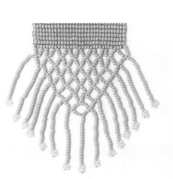

7 Continue, attaching a strand of fringe at left and right of each row, decreasing one mesh per row. Use one fewer bead when you make the final mesh. Insert needle into bead at center of that mesh and run it through beads, diagonally and upwards, until you reach right edge of first row of netting.

8 Tie and hide threads

● MAKING PICOTS AS YOU WEAVE

1 String beads for picots together with the beads for each horizontal row

2 Leaving the picot beads at the left edge, weave across the row as usual.

3 You now have a picot at the left edge of each woven row.

INSTRUCTIONS

For clarity, larger beads and darker thread have been used for the photographs of this section. The finished size stated for each piece is merely a benchmark and will vary depending on the specific beads used.

Some charts will instruct you to weave from top to bottom, and then bottom to top. When you work from them, rotate the book so that you are reading in the direction in which you are weaving.

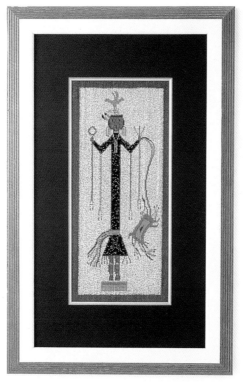

See Page 52 for instructions

[All projects will require the use of a loom and beading needles. Number 10 beading needles are suggested for the size 11 beads recommended. These are available in short (3.5mm), standard (6mm) and long (13mm) lengths. Where sewing is necessary, an ordinary sewing needle will be required. Other tools which might be required are listed with the specific project. Where glue is called for, a non-hardening fabric glue is suggested. For attachment of findings, a jewelers pliers will be required.]

BOUQUET BROOCH

Pictured on Page 16

Finished measurements: 4.5 cm x 11 cm
Thread: Gray
Supplies: Pin back (4.5 cm)
Warp: 32 threads
Vertical rows x Horizontal rows: 31 x 36
Fringe: Straight fringe (see Page 44)

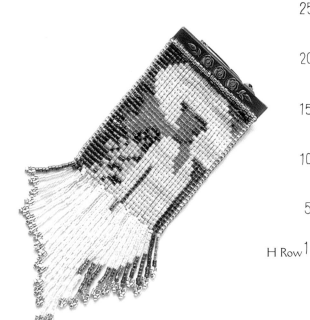

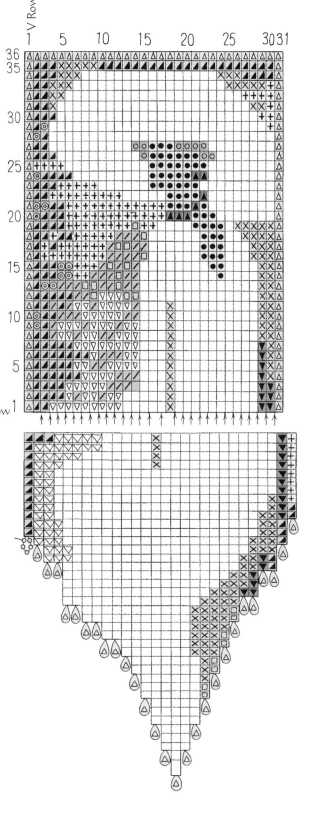

● INSTRUCTIONS

Weave brooch and hide threads. Be sure to make and attach the strands of fringe in the proper place, since they are part of the pattern. Attach pin back using about 50 cm of separate, double thread.

BEADS

□	= White Pearl	7g	○	= Brown iris	1g
▲	= Matte green	3g	╱	= Grass green	1g
▽	= Bright yellow	3g	✕	= Sky blue	1g
△	= Bright gold	3g	▼	= Blue luster	26 bds
●	= Light topaz	1g	▲	= Dark red	7 bds
▢	= Lilac	1g	◎	= Pearl peach	14 bds
+	= Lime	1g			

ATTACHING A PIN BACK

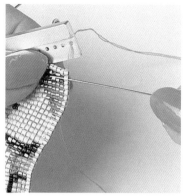

1 Hold woven piece and pin back in one hand. Thread a needle and insert it into the first hole in pin back, from the top. Pass needle through first bead in the second row, on the right edge.

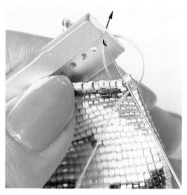

2 Pass the needle between the first and second beads on the first row, and back into the same hole on the pin back.

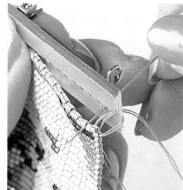

3 Pass the needle through the second hole on the pin back, from the bottom, and bring it out under the third bead on the first row.

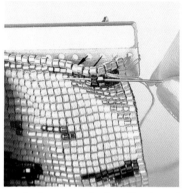

4 Insert needle into fourth and fifth beads on second row. Pass it under sixth and seventh beads on first row, and through third hole in pin back.

5 Repeat Steps 3 & 4 until you reach other edge of pin back. Photo shows view bottom of pin back.

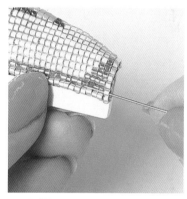

6 Turn piece over & pass needle through first bead on right side of 2nd row. Work as in Steps 3 & 4, passing needle through beads not picked up first time.

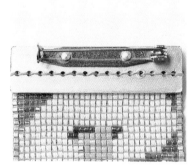

7 When you have traversed the piece the second time, there should be stitches between all the holes in the bottom of the pin back.

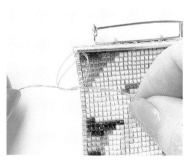

8 Tie threads together between the bottom of the pin back and the woven piece.

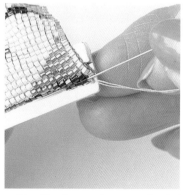

9 Use the needle to pass the tied threads through the beads under the bottom of the pin back and cut.

DIAMOND NECKLACE

Pictured on Page 26

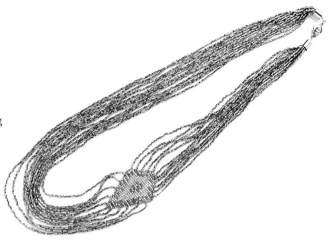

Finished measurements: 62 cm
Thread: Gray
Supplies: Cylindrical bail, 9-pin, jump ring
            (2 each), necklace clasp
Warp: 90 cm x 22 threads
Vertical rows x Horizontal rows: 21 x 30

● INSTRUCTIONS

Mark warp threads at a point measuring one-third their length, using a colored pencil. Warp loom. Begin forming diamond where you marked the threads, making increases and decreases for 30 rows. String beads on warp threads at left and right of the diamond, two threads at a time. Tie strands together. Attach bail, jump ring, and clasp (see Page 51).

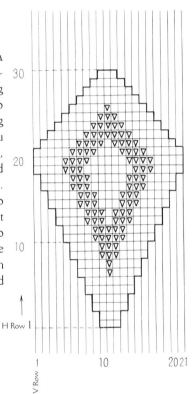

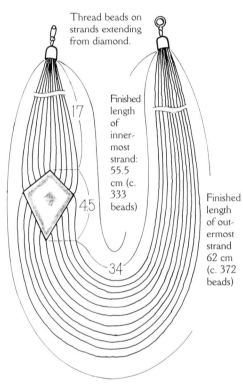

Thread beads on strands extending from diamond.

17

4.5

34

Finished length of innermost strand: 55.5 cm (c. 333 beads)

Finished length of outermost strand 62 cm (c. 372 beads)

BEADS

□	= Nickel (cut)	30g
▽	=Bright gld (cut)	2g

H Row 1

V Row 1

ATTACHING NECKLACE FINDINGS

METHOD A

1 Tie the thread to the circle on the 9-pin. Cut thread and apply carpenter's glue.

2 Insert the 9-pin into the cylindrical bail, and pull until the bail covers the end of the necklace.

3 Using pliers, cut the 9-pin, leaving 1 cm. Bend remainder to form a circle.

CHOKER

Pictured on Page 13

Finished measurements: 14 cm x 37 cm
Thread: Beige
Supplies: Bead tip (2), 9-pin, necklace clasp
Beads: 15 g bright silver (cut); 15 g silver (cut)
Warp: 80 cm x 45 threads
Vertical rows x Horizontal rows: 44 x 274

● INSTRUCTIONS

Weave Rows 1-137, mixing the two colors of beads, and increasing as shown in the chart. Work the pattern in Rows 138-163. From Row 164 to the end, weave in reverse, from Row 137 to Row 1. At the triangular openings, pull warp threads one at a time to form curves. Hide threads and attach findings.

STITCH CHART

Row		
1	①	1
2		3
62 ⌇	5	3
63		3
64		4
⌇	5	4
15 78		4
79		5
80		6
81		7
82		8
83		9
84		10
7 ⌇	5	10
90		10
91		13
8 ⌇		13
98		13
99	②	11
100	⑥	11
101	⑩	13
102	⑦	16
103	③	20
104		23
9 ⌇	5	23
112		23
113	②	21
114	⑥	17
115	⑩	13
116	⑬	10
117	⑦	6
118	⑭	19
119	①	22
120	⑦	26
121	③	30
122		33
11 ⌇	5	33
132		33
133	③	30
134	⑧	25
135	⑬	20
136	⑰	16
137	㉕	8

Row		
138	⑳	13x
139	⑮	18x
140	⑩ 6x 2•	16x
141	⑤ 6x 2• 3x 3•	16x
142	10x 4• 3x 3• 2x 1•	13x
143	9x 8• 1x 6•	13x
144	9x 9• 1x 6•	13x
145	10x 7• 4x 5•	13x
146	11x 3• 3• 4• 1x 4•	14x
147	14x 3• 1x 4• 1x 2• 4•	11x
148	13x 5• 2x 3• 2x 7•	10x
149	12x 1• 3x 4• 1x 3•	1x
150	9x 3• 1x 7• 1x 3• 1x 5•	14x
151	8x 3• 1x 8• 1x 3• 1x 4•	5x
152	7x 4• 1x 8• 1x 3• 1x 3•	15x
153	8x 3• 2x 6• 1• 1x 1• 1x 5•	13x
154	9x 3• 2x 4• 1x 3• 1x 6•	12x
155	8x 5• 2x 2• 1x 3• 2x 6•	11x
156	9x 5• 3x 3• 1x 1• 2x 4•	11x
157	4• 1x 2• 3x 4• 1x 2•	11x
158	11x 2• 1x 10•	13x
159	14x 9•	12x
160	⑤ 9x 9•	12x
161	⑩ 5x 2• 2x 4•	11x
162	⑮ 5x 2•	11x
163	⑳	13x

Rows 1-163
Rows 137-1

Unless otherwise indicated, mix the two colors of beads.

● = Bright silver (cut)
× = Silver (cut)

METHOD B

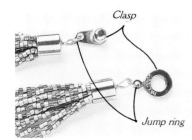

Clasp

Jump ring

4 Attach a jump ring between 9-pin and clasp.

1 Tie threads together and pass ends through a bead tip. Pass two strands of thread through a bead, tie, insert in bead tip. Close bead tip with pliers.

2 Bend the hook on the bead tip into a circle, add a jump ring, and then the other half of the clasp.

Tapestry or Framed Picture with Native American Motif

Pictured on Page 40

● TAPESTRY

Finished measurements: 17.5 cm x 49.5 cm
Thread: Gray
Supplies: Metal rod with gold finish (20 cm)
Beads: 15 g bright silver (cut); 15 g silver (cut)
Warp: 90 cm x 118 threads
Vertical rows x Horizontal rows: 117 x 258
Fringe: Straight fringe

● FRAMED PICTURE

Finished measurements: 17.5 cm x 38 cm
Thread: Gray
Supplies: Pasteboard (58 x 68 cm), frame
Beads: 15 g bright silver (cut); 15 g silver (cut)
Warp: 90 cm x 118 threads
Vertical rows x Horizontal rows: 117 x 226

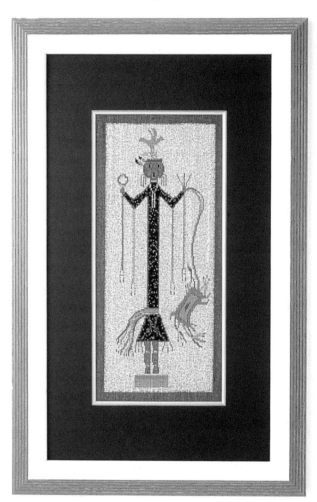

●INSTRUCTIONS

Weave the piece and hide threads. Sew down ends of straps at the top so that the tapestry can be mounted on a rod. String beads for the fringe in a wave pattern (see instructions on next page).

● INSTRUCTIONS

Weave in the same way as the tapestry, omitting the straps at top. Do not hide threads. Attach the woven piece to pasteboard.

FINISHING A TAPESTRY

1 Weave straps, following the chart on Page 59. Hide threads.

2 Fold straps toward back of woven piece. Using double thread, sew ends of straps down (see Page 42).

● ATTACHING THE FRINGE

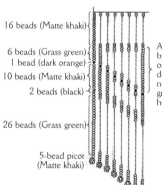

16 beads (Matte khaki)

6 beads (Grass green)
1 bead (dark orange)
10 beads (Matte khaki)
2 beads (black)

Alter length by increasing or decreasing number of green beads here.

In sections where there are 7 strands, omit the shortest strand of fringe.

26 beads (Grass green)

5-bead picot (Matte khaki)

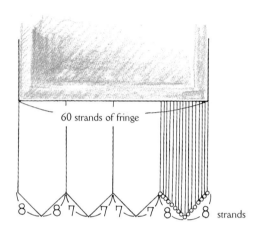

60 strands of fringe

8 8 7 7 7 7 8 8 strands

FRAMING A WOVEN PIECE

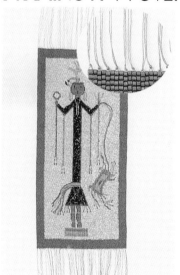

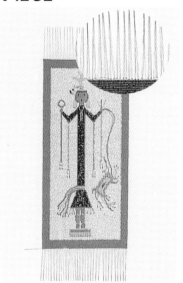

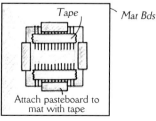

Tape — Mat Bds

Attach pasteboard to mat with tape

1 Remove woven piece from the loom. Tie warp threads together in pairs, at the edge of the woven piece.

2 Use a sheet of pasteboard 10 cm larger than sides of the woven piece. Cut vertical 5-mm slits into the top and bottom of the pasteboard, spacing them 5mm apart, and insert the tied warp threads into them.

3 Cut the threads to a length of 5 cm at the back, and tape them down. Place mounted woven piece on mat and attach with tape.

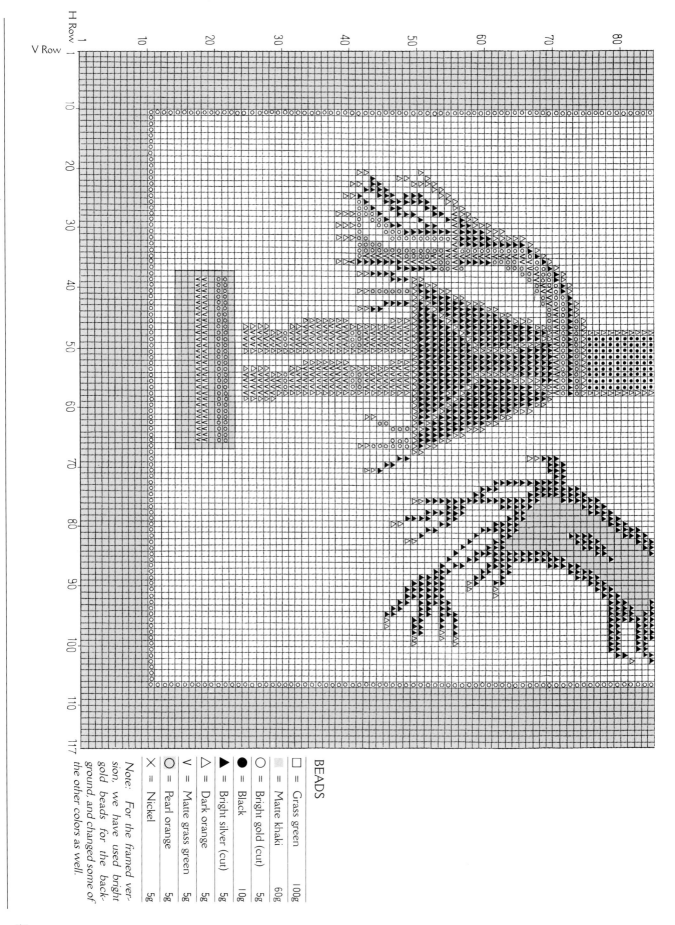

BEADS

□	=	Grass green	100g
▦	=	Matte khaki	60g
○	=	Bright gold (cut)	5g
○	=	Bright gold (cut)	10g
▲	=	Black	5g
●	=	Bright silver (cut)	5g
△	=	Dark orange	5g
V	=	Matte grass green	5g
◯	=	Pearl orange	5g
✕	=	Nickel	5g

Note: For the framed version, we have used bright gold beads for the background, and changed some of the other colors as well.

54

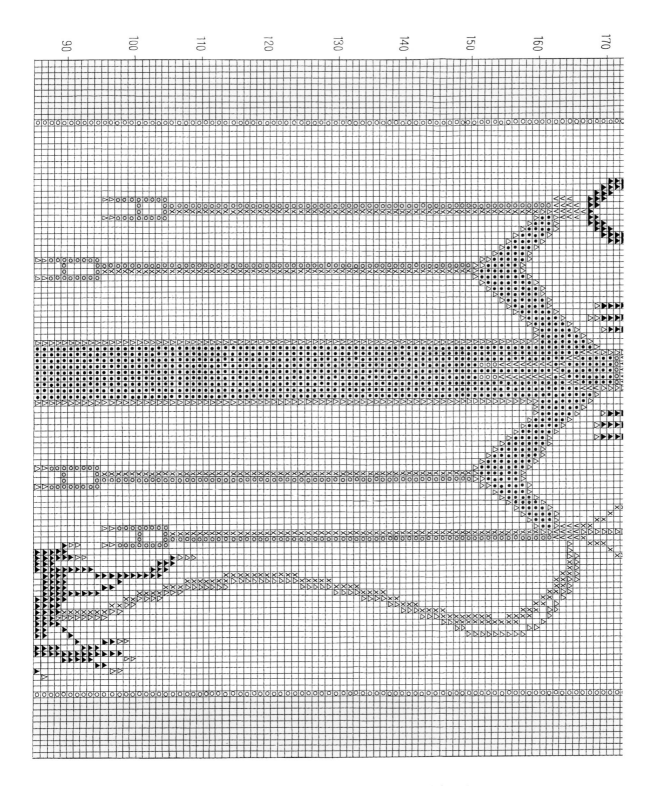

CHART FOR
TAPESTRY
WITH NATIVE
AMERICAN
MOTIF

Continued on Page 59

Rose Corsage

Pictured on Page 33

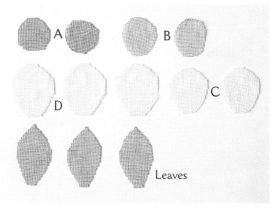

1 Using transparent beads and red, pink, white, and green thread, weave the flower petals and leaves.

Finished measurements:
   9 cm (diameter)
Thread: Red, pink, white, green
Supplies: lengths 28-gauge wire (30 cm each), corsage finding or perforated pin back
Beads: Transparent (60 g)

● Assembling the Corsage on a Corsage Finding

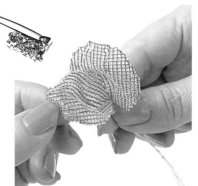

1 Twist the wires together at the bases of the petals. Make sure that the small red petals are facing each other.

2 With the red petals forming the center, arrange the pink and white petals around them, starting with small, and ending with large petals.

6 Wrap wire around end of receptacle on corsage pin and cut.

7 Insert a piece of fabric into corsage pin, as shown above. Grasp fabric and receptacle with pliers and compress.

● Instructions

Weave nine petals and three leaves, using transparent beads and four colors of thread, following the charts on Page 58. Then follow the directions on this page and the next.

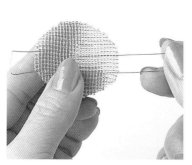

2 Shape a piece of wire in a hairpin shape with 1 cm spacing. Run the wire through petal, bending it as you go.

3 Shape the wire with your fingertips to form the petals.

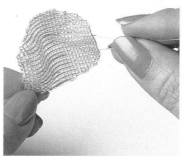

4 Spread a thin coat of carpenter's glue over the back of the petal.

3 Arrange the leaves around the petals. Wind a wire from one of the leaves around the other wires at the bottom of the corsage.

4 Cut all but one wire to a length of 2 cm. Wind that wire around the others. Fold the other wires in half.

5 Insert folded wire into the opening of the receptacle on the corsage finding. Pass remaining wire through holes in finding two or three times.

● ASSEMBLING THE CORSAGE ON A PERFORATED PIN BACK

1 After running the wire through the first petal, insert it into a hole at the center of the pin back.

2 Shape petals and leaves, and insert wires into the pin back, working from center out. Gather up all wires, cut, and twist.

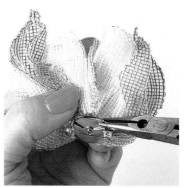

3 Attach base of pin back, bend down tabs, and tighten with pliers.

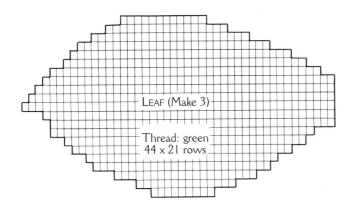

LEAF (Make 3)

Thread: green
44 x 21 rows

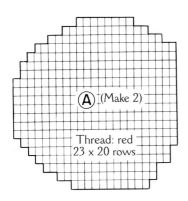

Ⓐ (Make 2)

Thread: red
23 x 20 rows

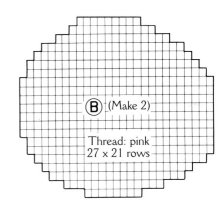

Ⓑ (Make 2)

Thread: pink
27 x 21 rows

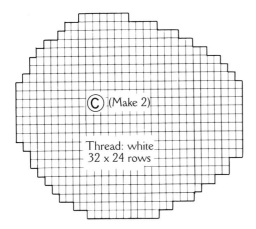

Ⓒ (Make 2)

Thread: white
32 x 24 rows

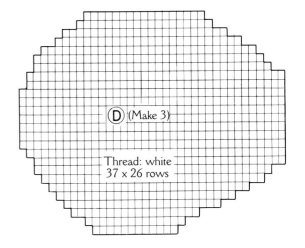

Ⓓ (Make 3)

Thread: white
37 x 26 rows

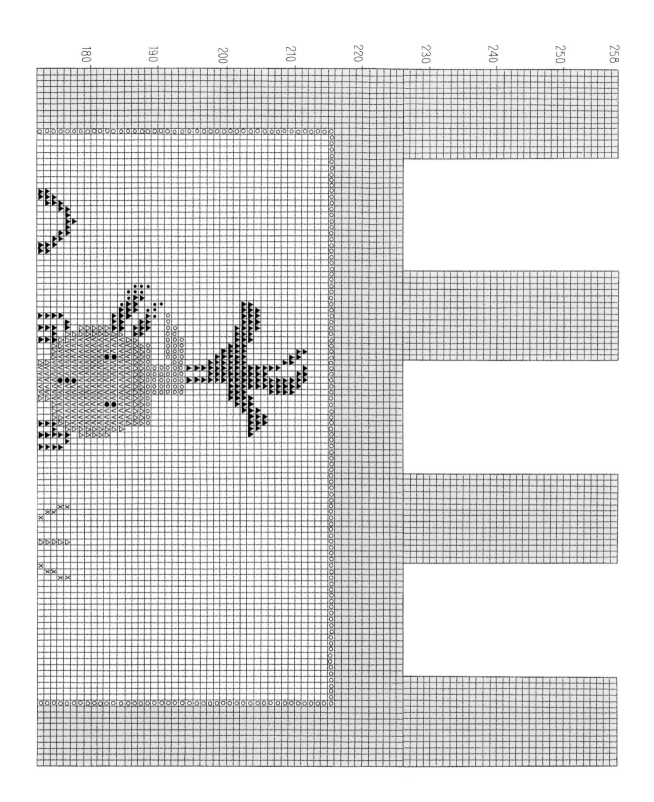

180 190 200 210 220 230 240 250 258

CHART FOR
TAPESTRY
WITH NATIVE
AMERICAN
MOTIF

Instructions on Page 52

ALPHABET BAG

Pictured on Page 15

Finished measurements: 14 cm x 20 cm
Thread: Black
Supplies: black (or brown) fabric for lining
             and interfacing (20 x 50 cm each),
             zipper (11 cm)
Warp: 90 cm x 94 threads
             180 cm x 16 threads for strap (warp
             with double thread)
Vertical rows x Horizontal rows: 93 x 205
Fringe: Straight fringe (see Page 44)

● INSTRUCTIONS

For front of bag, weave the stripes and the letters A-G; for the back, weave only the stripes. Hide the threads, and join sides. Work 94 strands of fringe, forming stripes and the letters "H" and "I". To provide added strength, warp the loom with double thread for the strap. For the black bag, weave stripes into the strap, working on 7 beads for about 120 cm. Attach the strap to both sides of the bag. Attach lining.

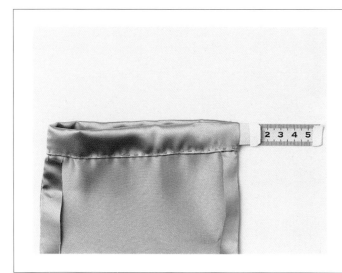

● INSERTING STEEL BONING

For the boning, cut a section of a retractable steel tape measure to the desired length. Tape the cut edges. Fold top edge of lining over twice and sew to form a casing. Insert section of tape measure and sew opening. Insert lining into bag. Attach as you would a zipper.

ATTACHING A ZIPPER

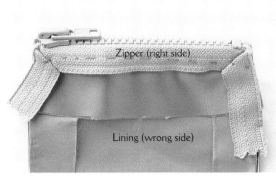

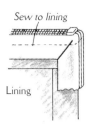

Fold down the end of the zipper and sew, forming a corner.

Sew to lining

Lining

1 Fold zipper over the center of the top edge of the lining and sew as shown above.

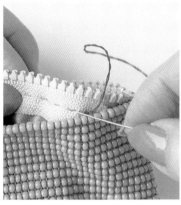

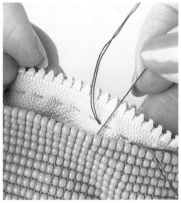

2 Insert lining into the bag. Using double thread, insert a needle into the line of stitches on the zipper from underneath.

3 Pick up 1 cm of the zipper fabric, and bring the needle out in the second row of the woven piece.

4 Pass the needle through two beads on the second row, and then back into the zipper. Repeat Steps 3 and 4.

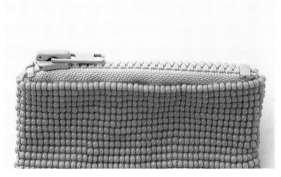

5 Make sure that your stitches do not go through to the right side of the lining

6 This is how the bag should look once the zipper has been attached.

● CUTTING THE LINING

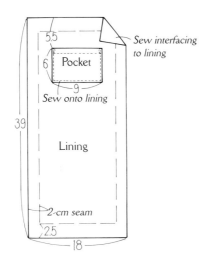

Sew interfacing to lining

5.5
6 Pocket
9
Sew onto lining
39
Lining
2-cm seam
2.5
18

● SEWING THE LINING

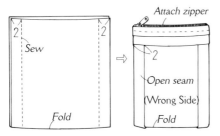

Attach zipper

2 / 2
Sew
Fold

2
Open seam
(Wrong Side)
Fold

Fold inside out and sew together at edges.

● SEWING THE LINING

1 Cut out the lining to measure 5 cm longer and 4 cm wider than the woven piece. Sew interface to lining and iron.

2 Cut out the pocket, turn edges under, and sew onto lining.

3 Fold lining in half, wrong side out. Sew together at both edges. Open seams.

4 Attach a zipper to the lining, or make a casing and insert steel boning.

5 Attach the lining to the woven piece 5 mm from teeth of the zipper (at the edge when using steel boning).

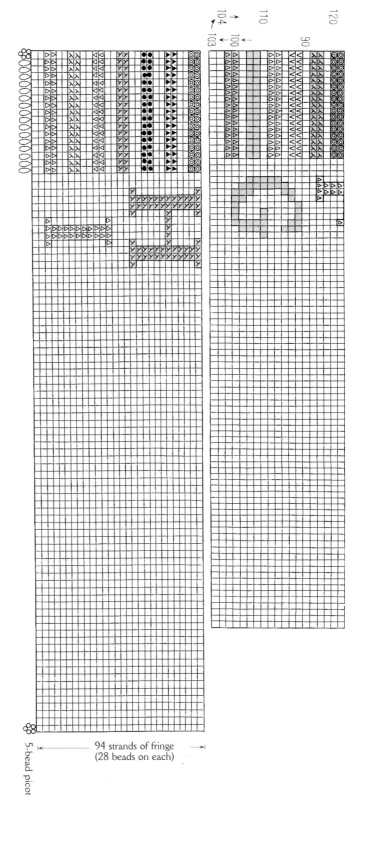

5-bead picot

94 strands of fringe (28 beads on each)

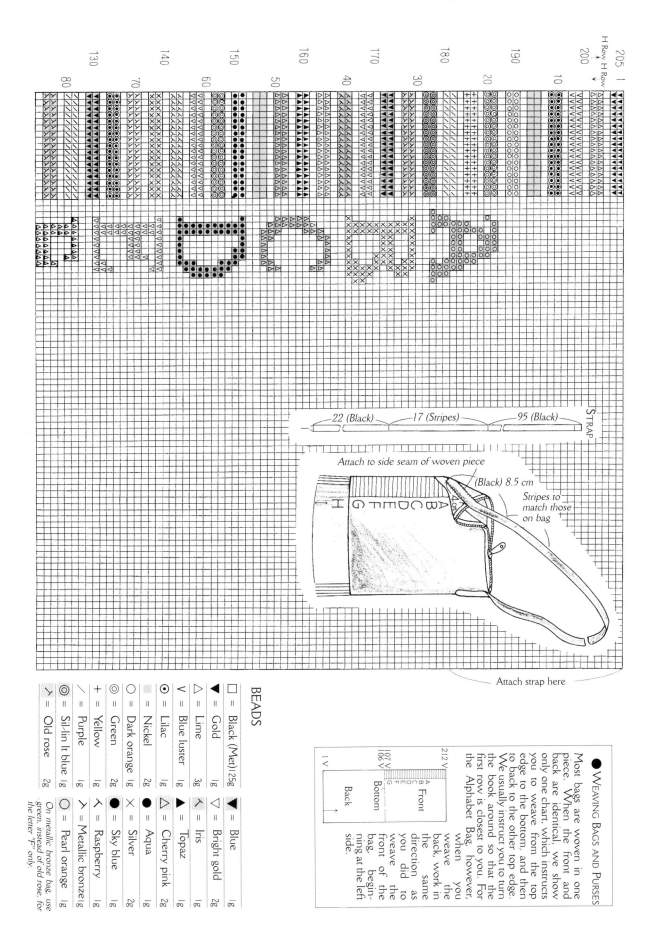

Attach to side seam of woven piece

22 (Black) — *17 (Stripes)* — *95 (Black)*

STRAP

(Black) 8.5 cm

Stripes to match those on bag

Attach strap here

● WEAVING BAGS AND PURSES

Most bags are woven in one piece. When the front and back are identical, we show only one chart, which instructs you to weave from the top edge to the bottom, and then to back to the other top edge. We usually instruct you to turn the book around so that the first row is closest to you. For the Alphabet Bag, however,

when you weave the back, work in the same direction as you did to weave the front of the bag, beginning at the left side.

212 V		
	A Front	
107 V	B	
106 V	C D E F G Bottom	
1 V		Back

BEADS

□	= Black (Met)	25g	◢	= Blue	1g
◀	= Gold	1g	▷	= Bright gold	1g
△	= Lime	3g	⅄	= Iris	1g
∨	= Blue luster	1g	▽	= Topaz	1g
⊙	= Lilac	1g	◮	= Cherry pink	2g
●	= Nickel	2g	▶	= Aqua	1g
○	= Dark orange	1g	✕	= Silver	2g
◎	= Green	2g	●	= Sky blue	1g
/	= Yellow	1g	⅄	= Raspberry	1g
+	= Purple	1g	⅄	= Metallic bronze	1g
◎	= Sil-lin lt blue	2g	○	= Pearl orange	1g
⅄	= Old rose	2g			

On metallic bronze bag, use green, instead of old rose, for the letter "F" only.

63

BAG WITH ARABESQUE MOTIF

Pictured on Page 26

Finished measurements: 17.5 cm x 24.5 cm
Thread: Gray
Supplies: White fabric for lining (22 x 42 cm)
Warp: 90 cm x 116 threads
          90 cm x 10 threads for strap
Vertical rows x Horizontal rows: 115 x 239
Fringe: Criss-cross fringe (see Page 44)

SHAPING

INSTRUCTIONS

Form slits in Rows 16-22. Begin decreasing on Row 104. When you reach Row 120, weave in reverse order, ending with Row 239. Pull warp threads to shape bottom of bag. Hide warp threads in the beads underneath the slits. Make 5-bead picots on the bottom of the bag, as shown on Page 66. Attach criss-cross fringe between picots. Make 5-bead picots at the opening of the bag as well. Using double warp thread, weave two 4-bead, 120-row straps. Run them through slits and join.

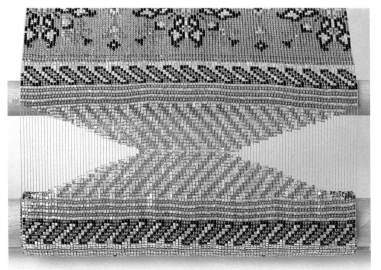

SHAPING THE BOTTOM OF THE BAG

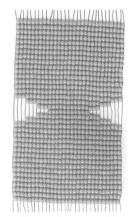

1   Shape bottom of bag, making increases and decreases as shown in chart. Increase and decrease so that the threads are not visible.

FORMING SLITS

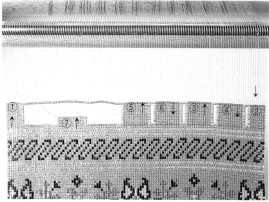

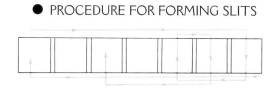

● PROCEDURE FOR FORMING SLITS

1. First, weave the sections at both edges. Then proceed to next row of the next slit. Proceed from Section 1 to Section 8, following the arrows in the photograph above, rotating the loom when appropriate.

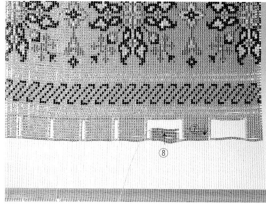

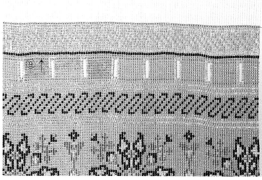

2. For instance, when you have woven Section 7, rotate the loom, pass the needle through the beads at the top, bring it out at the left edge of Section 8, and then weave Section 8.

3. For Section 9, pass needle through bottom row of slit, bring it out at left edge of Section 9, and weave Section 9 in same way you worked Section 7. Pass needle through next row of slit, bring it out on left edge, and continue weaving opening of the bag.

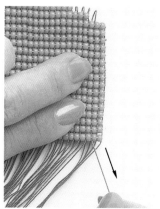

2. Remove the piece from the loom. Fold it in half, and pull on the warp threads, one at a time.

3. This is how the piece should look when you have pulled all the threads on one side.

4. This is how the piece should look when you have pulled the threads on both sides.

● CUTTING THE LINING

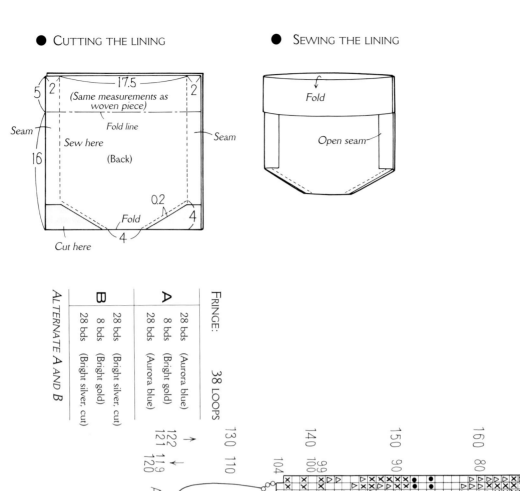

17.5
5 2 (Same measurements as woven piece) 2

Fold line

Seam ——— Sew here ——— Seam
(Back)

16

0.2

Fold

4

4

Cut here

● SEWING THE LINING

Fold

Open seam

FRINGE: 38 LOOPS

A	28 bds	(Aurora blue)
	8 bds	(Bright gold)
	28 bds	(Aurora blue)
B	28 bds	(Bright silver, cut)
	8 bds	(Bright gold)
	28 bds	(Bright silver, cut)

ALTERNATE A AND B

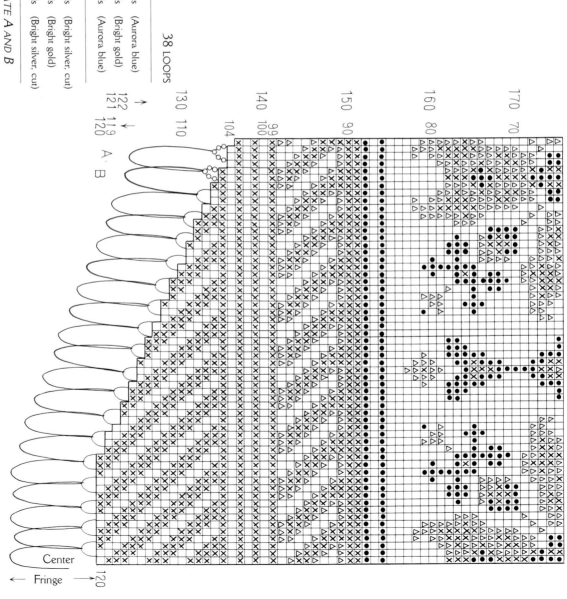

122
121
120 119

A.
B

130 110
104
99
100
90
80
70

140
150
160
170

Center

← Fringe → 120

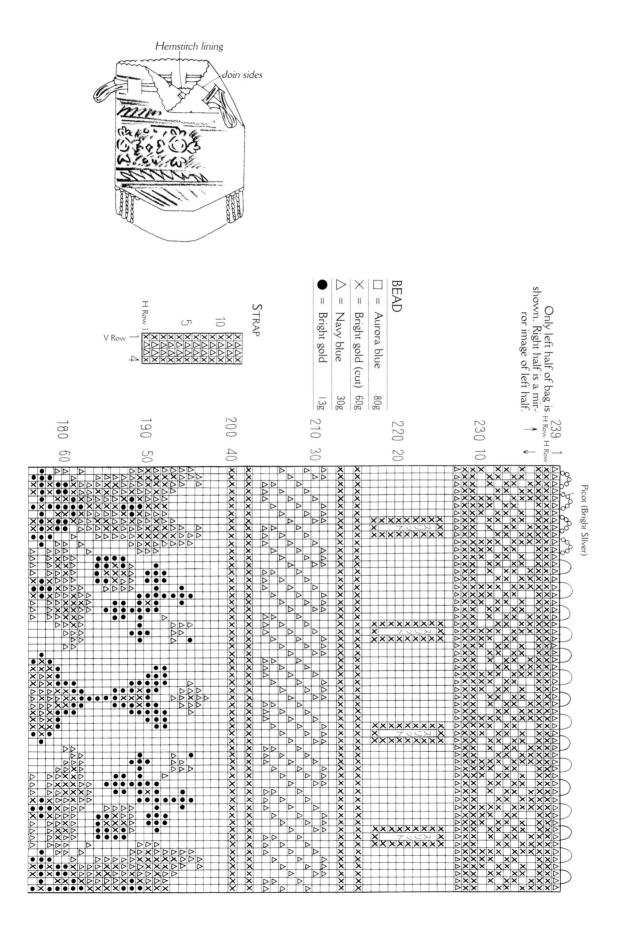

Hemstitch lining

Join sides

Only left half of bag is
shown. Right half is a mir-
ror image of left half.

239 1 H Row H Row
            H Row

BEAD

□ = Aurora blue   80g
✕ = Bright gold (cut)   60g
△ = Navy blue   30g
● = Bright gold   13g

STRAP

Picot (Bright Silver)

PURSE WITH TINY ROSES

Pictured on Page 22

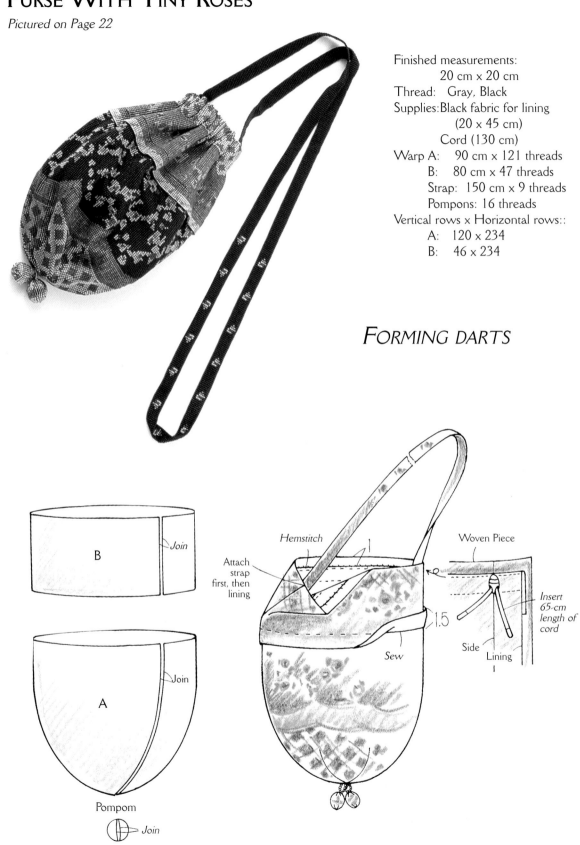

Finished measurements:
       20 cm x 20 cm
Thread: Gray, Black
Supplies: Black fabric for lining
       (20 x 45 cm)
       Cord (130 cm)
Warp A: 90 cm x 121 threads
     B: 80 cm x 47 threads
   Strap: 150 cm x 9 threads
   Pompons: 16 threads
Vertical rows x Horizontal rows::
     A: 120 x 234
     B: 46 x 234

FORMING DARTS

B

Join

A

Join

Pompom

Join

Hemstitch

Attach
strap
first, then
lining

Woven Piece

1.5

Sew

Insert
65-cm
length of
cord

Side   Lining

● INSTRUCTIONS

Use black thread for A and the strap, and gray thread for B and the pompoms. For A and B, weave from Row 1 to Row 78; repeat twice. On A, pull the threads at the darts to shape the bottom of the pouch. Join the first and last rows of A (see Method A on Page 42. Join the 10th bead on A to the right edge of B. To make the strap, weave 720 rows of eight beads. Attach 25 rows of strap to each side of pouch. Weave pompoms, stuff with cotton batting, and attach to bottom center of pouch. Sew lining, following directions on this page, insert into pouch, and attach. Run cord through casing. (See Page 42 for tips on joining woven pieces.)

● SEWING THE LINING

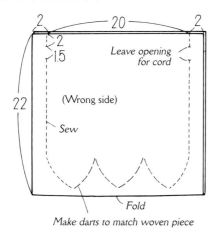

Make darts to match woven piece

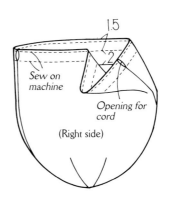

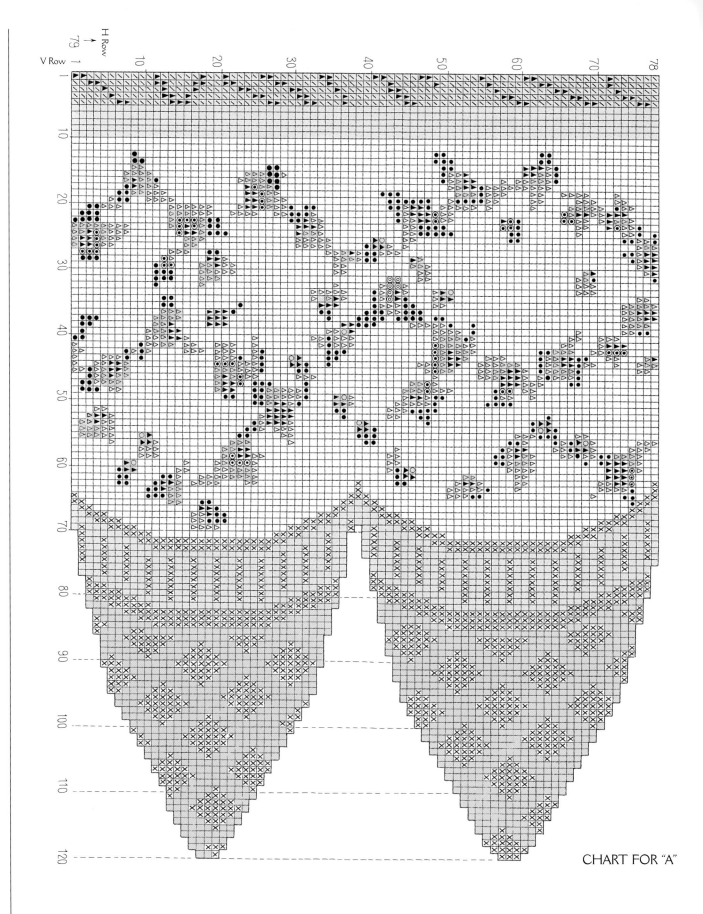

CHART FOR "A"

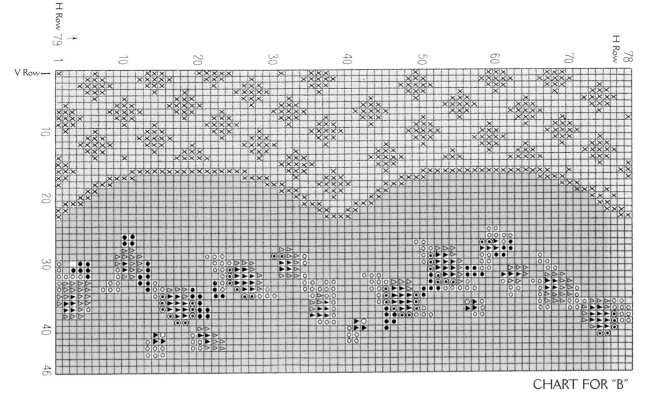

CHART FOR "B"

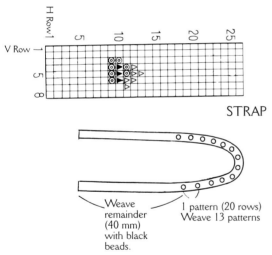

STRAP

Weave remainder (40 mm) with black beads.

1 pattern (20 rows)
Weave 13 patterns

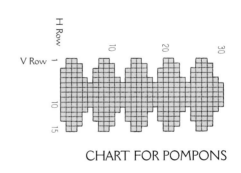

CHART FOR POMPONS

□	=	Matte black	80g
▨	=	Matte gray	60g
▧	=	Nickel luster	40g
╱	=	Light gray	10g
✕	=	Matte wine	25g
△	=	Grass green	10g
●	=	Lime	7g
○	=	Green	5g
▶	=	Raspberry luster	5g
◁	=	Lilac	5g
⊙	=	Magenta	5g
○	=	Cherry pink	10 bds
▲	=	Shell pink	36 bds

BAG WITH EGYPTIAN MOTIFS

Pictured on Page 29

Finished measurements: 21.5 cm x 13.5 cm
Thread: Gray
Supplies: Two pieces white fabric for lining and
          interfacing (20 x 45 cm each),
          gold purse frame (17 cm x 4 cm),
          gold chain (70 cm)
Warp: 90 cm x 146 threads
Vertical rows x Horizontal rows: 145 x 163

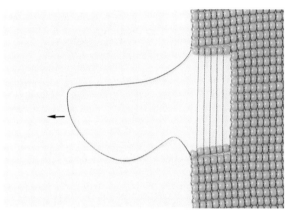

2 Remove woven piece from loom. Pull warp threads inside the cutouts at each edge of the bottom of piece, one at a time.

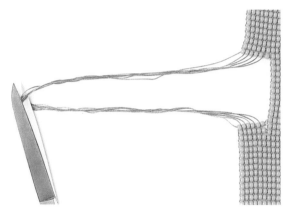

3 When you have pulled the threads to a length of 20 cm, cut at center.

JOINING

6 Fold the cutout, and insert threaded needle into point marked "A" in Step 5. Pick up two beads.

7 Pick up warp and weft threads every other row.

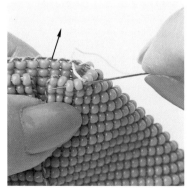

8 Repeat Steps 6 and 7 until you reach the edge.

FORMING THE CUTOUTS

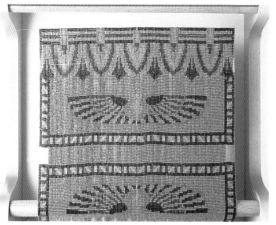

1   When you shape the bottom of the bag, increase and decrease at left and right, forming rectangular "cutouts" at each side of the woven piece.

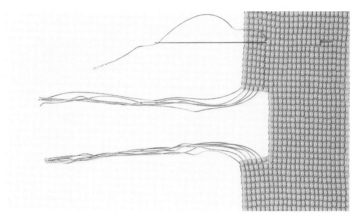

4   Hide the cut warp threads by running them through 2 cm of weft threads and then through several beads.

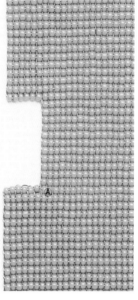

5   This is how the piece should look when you have finished hiding the threads.

9   Turn the piece around and pick up weft and warp threads skipped the first time.

10   Work across, picking up two beads at a time, beginning with a bead not picked up the first time.

11   When you return to A, work back to center. Join edges.

● INSTRUCTIONS

Weave Rows 1-76. Between Rows 77 and 88, decrease seven beads at each side to form rectangular space. Starting in Row 89, weave back to Row 1, for a total of 164 rows. Attach purse frame, lining (see Pages 76-80), and chain.

Attach lining to purse frame

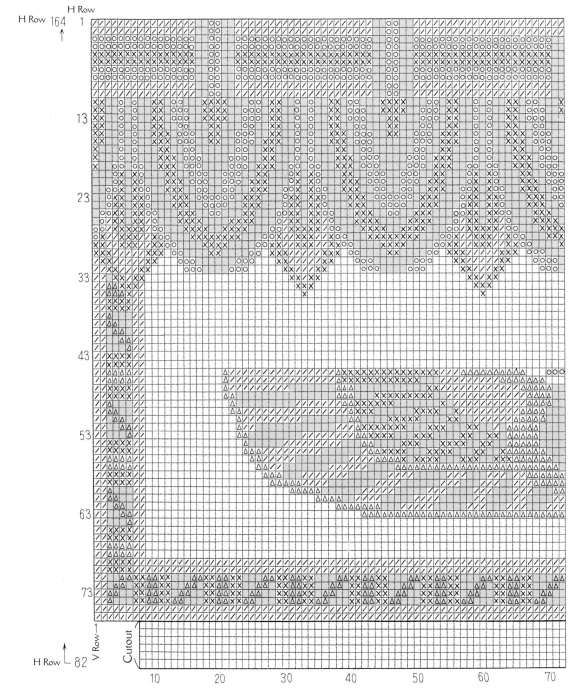

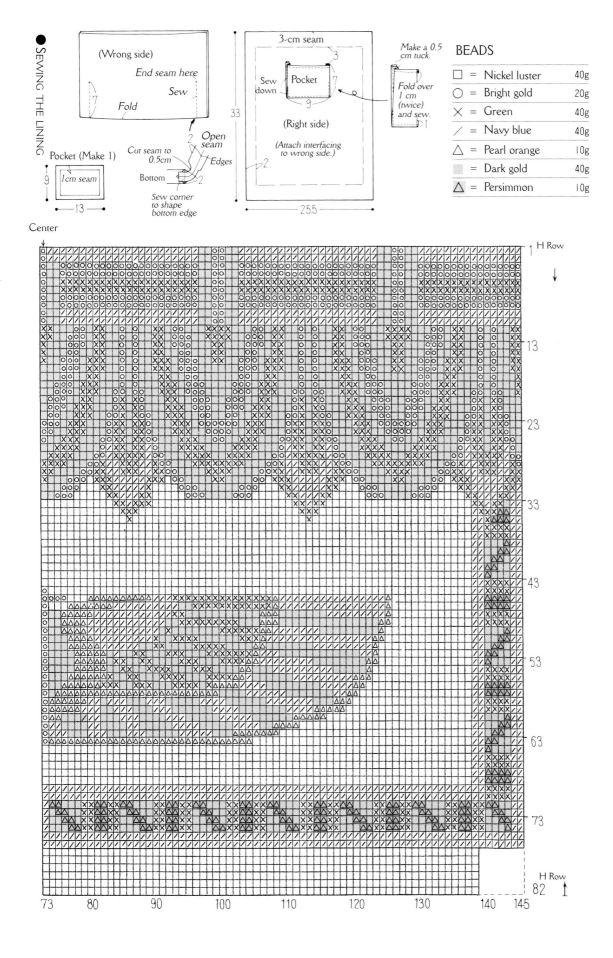

● SEWING THE LINING

(Wrong side)

End seam here

Sew

Fold

Pocket (Make 1)

1cm seam

9

— 13 —

Cut seam to
0.5cm

2

*Open
seam*

Edges

Bottom

2

Sew corner
to shape
bottom edge

33

3-cm seam

3

Sew
down

Pocket

9

(Right side)

(Attach interfacing
to wrong side.)

2

— 25.5 —

Make a 0.5
cm tuck.

Fold over
1 cm
(twice)
and sew.

1

BEADS

□	=	Nickel luster	40g
○	=	Bright gold	20g
×	=	Green	40g
/	=	Navy blue	40g
△	=	Pearl orange	10g
▨	=	Dark gold	40g
△	=	Persimmon	10g

Center

1 H Row

13

23

33

43

53

63

73

H Row
82

73   80   90   100   110   120   130   140 145

SILVER PURSE WITH FRINGE

Pictured on Page 13

Finished measurements: 15 cm x 21.5 cm

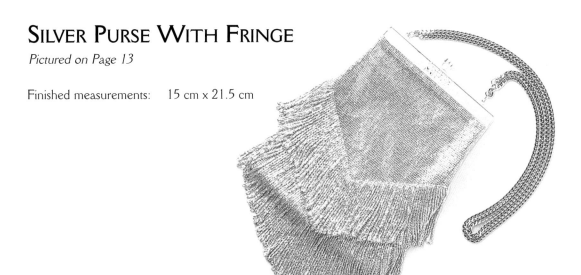

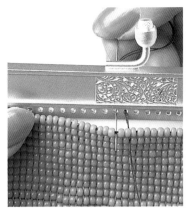

3 Pass needle through next hole in the purse frame to the left, from back. Skip two beads, and bring needle out under weft thread in top row of beads.

4 Pick up two beads on the second row.

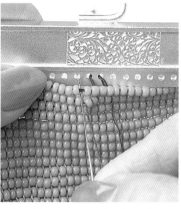

5 Pass the needle through the next hole to the left, going underneath the weft thread on the top row.

9 Pick up the warp threads skipped the first time and work as before, until you have reached the other side of the purse frame.

10 Pick up the warp thread on the second row, and insert the needle into the uppermost hole in the purse frame, from the front.

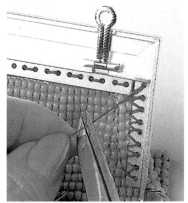

11 Attach the thread at the back of the purse frame into the warp thread at the edge of the woven piece, tie it in a square knot, and cut.

ATTACHING THE PURSE FRAME
(CHOOSE FRAME THAT IS 1-1.5 CM NARROWER THAN WOVEN PIECE)

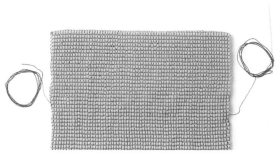

1 Fold the woven piece in half. Cut a strand of thread measuring about 180 cm, and sew the sides together. Leave sides open at top of bag to accommodate height of purse frame + 1 cm. Do not cut the thread, because you will use it to attach the lining.

2 Center purse frame at the top of woven bag. From the second row of beads, pass a needle through the hole at the center of purse frame. Sew woven piece to purse frame, using double thread (200 cm), working from center to one side and then the other.

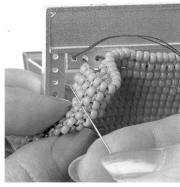

6 Repeat Steps 3-5 until you are 1 cm from edge of purse frame. Fold edge of woven piece under, pick up warp thread from third row, and insert needle into top left hole in the purse frame.

7 Insert needle into next hole in purse frame, from back. Pick up the warp thread under the second row at the edge of the folded woven piece.

8 Repeat Step 7. Pick up the warp and weft threads at the edge of the woven piece.

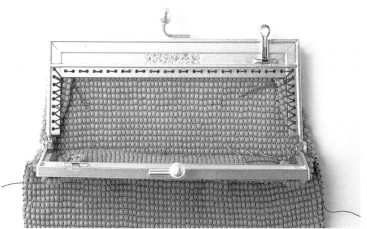

12 Work the right half in the same way, using the remaining thread.

Thread: Beige
Supplies: Two pieces white fabric for lining and interfacing (20 x 50 cm each), silver purse frame (12 cm x 4 cm), silver chain (100 cm)
Warp: 90 cm x 101 threads
Vertical rows x Horizontal rows: 100 x 209
Fringe: Straight fringe (see Page 44)

● CUTTING OUT THE LINING

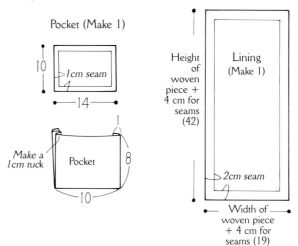

Pocket (Make 1)

1cm seam
10
14

Make a 1cm tuck
Pocket
8
10

Height of woven piece + 4 cm for seams (42)

Lining (Make 1)

2cm seam

Width of woven piece + 4 cm for seams (19)

● INSTRUCTIONS

Place the silver cut and bright silver cut beads in a container and mix them well. Weave 209 rows on 100 beads without increasing or decreasing. Hide threads and join sides. Make two rows of straight fringe, forming a "V", and attach to both sides of purse. Attach purse frame to bag, following instructions on Page 76. Sew the pocket to the lining, and sew lining to the woven piece (see Page 80). Attach chain.

● SEWING THE LINING

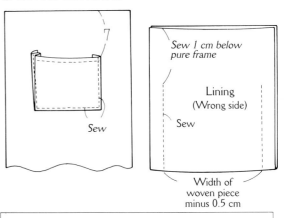

Sew

Sew 1 cm below pure frame

Lining (Wrong side)

Sew

Width of woven piece minus 0.5 cm

● SEWING THE LINING OF A BAG WITH A PURSE FRAME ATTACHED

1 Cut a piece of fabric 4 cm larger, on all sides, than the woven piece.

2 Cut fabric for pocket, allowing 1 cm for seams. No interfacing is necessary. Make a tuck in one side, fold seams under and machine-sew to lining.

3 Fold lining in half lengthwise. Sew sides, leaving a 2-cm seam on each. Stop 1 cm below the point where the purse frame will be attached.

4 Press seams open.

Note: Since the size of the woven piece will differ from weaver to weaver, measure it after you remove it from loom.

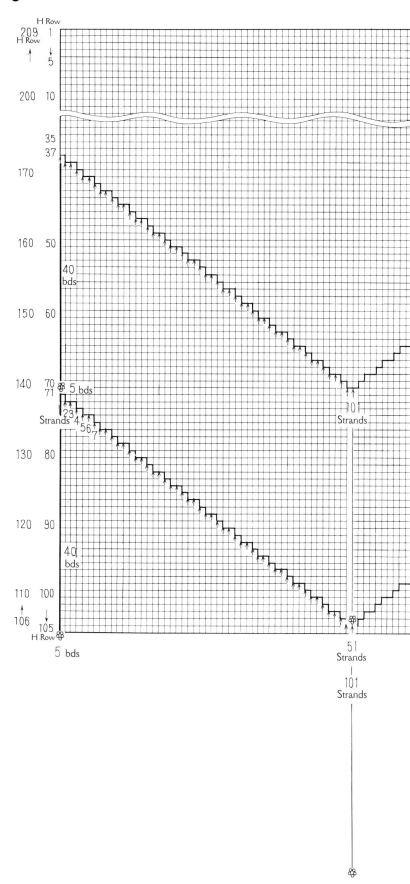

ATTACHING A LINING TO A BAG WITH A PURSE FRAME

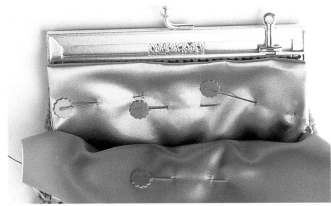

1 Sew the lining and insert into woven piece to which purse frame has been attached. Make sure that bottoms of lining and woven piece are aligned properly. Fasten lining and woven piece with marking pins. Fold seams inward, aligning the folds with the purse frame. Fasten with marking pins.

2 Open purse frame wide. Join portions of lining and woven piece not attached to purse frame, gathering the lining as necessary. Thread a needle with the reserved thread, and make a tiny stitch on the lining from the fold.

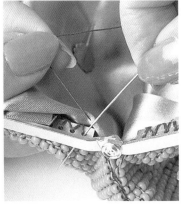

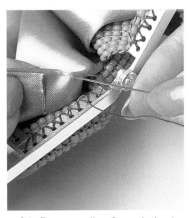

3 Pick up a warp thread. Repeat Steps 2 and 3.

4 When you reach the purse frame, pass the needle through a hole in it from the wrong side of the lining.

5 Pass needle from hole in purse frame into wrong side of lining 1mm from seam. Continue working, aligning stitches so that lining lies properly.

6 Repeat Steps 4 and 5 until you reach the opposite edge of the purse frame. Then, join the lining to the portion of the woven piece not attached to the purse frame.

7 Join lining to other side of bag in the same way.

BROOCH AND EARRINGS WITH TRIANGLE MOTIF

Pictured on Page 7

BROOCH

Finished measurements: 4.7 cm x 7 cm
Thread: Gray
Supplies: Pin back (4.5 cm)
Warp: 31 threads
Horizontal rows x
    vertical rows:
        13 x 30
Fringe: Straight fringe
    (see Page 44)

EARRINGS

Finished measurements: 1.5 cm x 3 cm
Thread: Gray
Supplies: Two bead tips, two jump rings, set of
        earring backs
Warp: 11 threads
Vertical rows x Horizontal rows:
        10 x 18

● INSTRUCTIONS

Weave brooch and hide threads. Thread a needle with about 80 cm of thread. Attach fringe, following the chart and working from the left side. Attach pin back (see Page 49).

BEADS

□	= Nickel	2g
▲	= Matte charcoal gray	3g
╱	= Silver (cut)	1g
△	= Bright silver (cut)	1g
▨	= Black (cut)	2g
○	= Transparent (cut)	1g
◎	= Crystal	1g

● INSTRUCTIONS

Make two of the woven pieces. With separate, double thread, attach a bead tip to the bead in the upper right corner of each woven piece (see Page 51). Attach jump ring to bead tip and earring back.

BEADS

□	= Nickel	1g
▨	= Black	2g
✕	= Charcoal gray (cut)	1g
△	= Light rhodium	1g

CHART FOR BROOCH

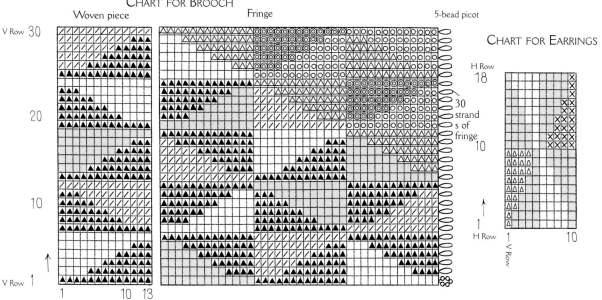

CHART FOR EARRINGS

SHOULDER BAG WITH TRIANGLE MOTIF

Pictured on Page 6

Finished measurements: 14 cm x 22 cm
Tools: Loom, needle, sewing needle
Thread: Black
Supplies: Two pieces black fabric for lining and
        interfacing (20 x 50 cm each), two lengths
        of steel boning (13 cm each)
Warp: 90 cm x 97 threads
Vertical rows x Horizontal rows: 96 x 292
Fringe: Straight fringe (see Page 44)

● INSTRUCTIONS

Weave the front and back of the bag (Rows 1 through 209). On Row 210, decrease 12 beads at left and right for the flap. Continue to decrease on both sides, forming a triangle. Hide threads, sew sides together, and attach fringe to the bottom of the bag and the end of the flap. Attach lining and insert steel boning (see Page 60).

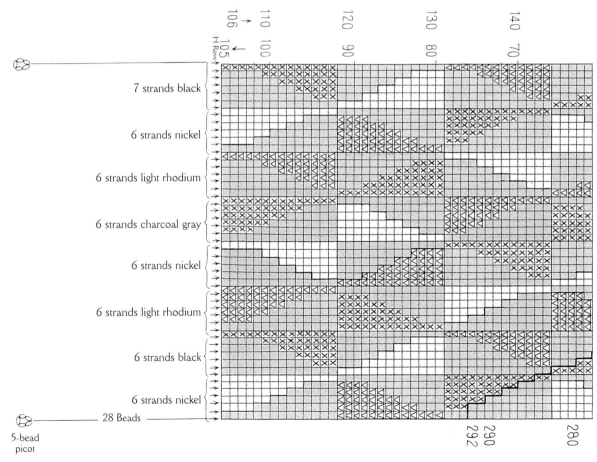

7 strands black

6 strands nickel

6 strands light rhodium

6 strands charcoal gray

6 strands nickel

6 strands light rhodium

6 strands black

6 strands nickel

— 28 Beads —

5-bead picot

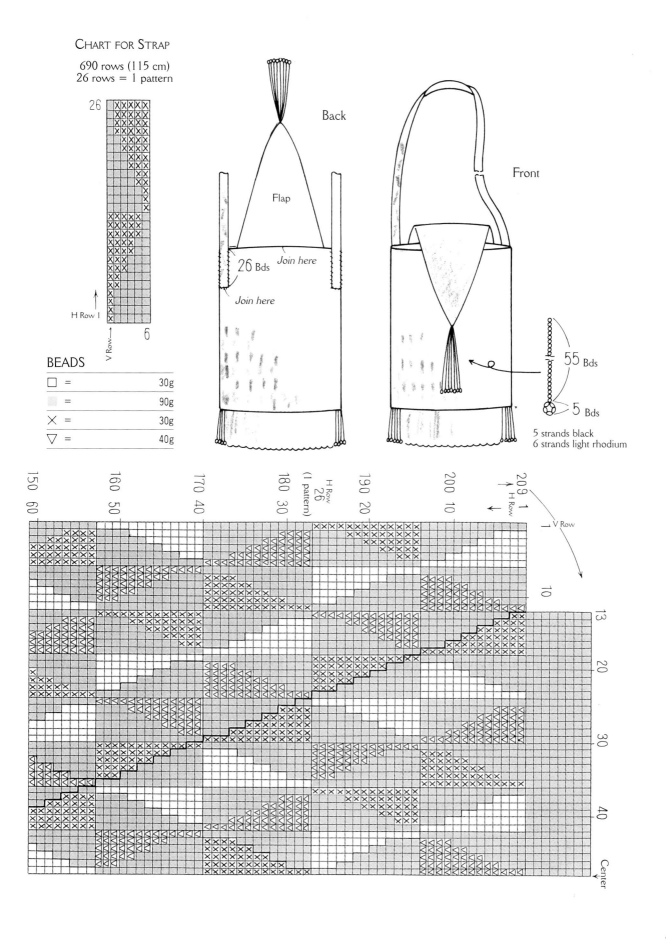

CHART FOR STRAP

690 rows (115 cm)
26 rows = 1 pattern

26

H Row 1

V Row

6

Back

Flap

Join here

26 Bds

Join here

Front

55 Bds

5 Bds

5 strands black
6 strands light rhodium

BEADS

□	=	30g
▦	=	90g
×	=	30g
▽	=	40g

150 60
160 50
170 40
180 30
(1 pattern)
H Row 26
190 20
200 10
209 1
H Row
V Row
1
10

13
20
30
40
Center

BAG AND BELT WITH DIAMOND MOTIF

Pictured on Page 8

BAG

Finished measurements: 14 cm x 19 cm
Thread: Black
Supplies: Two pieces black fabric for
lining and interfacing
(20 x 50 cm each),
gray zipper (12.5 cm)
Warp: 90 cm x 99 threads
Vertical rows x Horizontal rows: 98 x 223
Fringe: Twisted fringe (see Page 44)

● INSTRUCTIONS

Weave bag, hide threads, and sew sides together. Attach fringe. Attach lining and zipper (see Pages 61). Join 25 rows of the strap to each side.

BELT

Finished measurements: 5 cm x 85 cm
(waist measurement + 20 cm)
Thread: Black
Supplies: Belt buckle (5 cm)
Warp: (Length + 30 cm) x 70 threads
(use double thread)
Vertical rows x Horizontal rows:
34 x (multiple of 16 rows)

● INSTRUCTIONS

Warp loom with double thread for added strength. Make increases from Rows 1-8, until you have 34 beads. Weave on 34 beads until piece reaches a length equivalent to waist measurement + 20 cm. Attach buckle. See Page 42 for instructions on joining woven pieces.

CHART FOR BELT

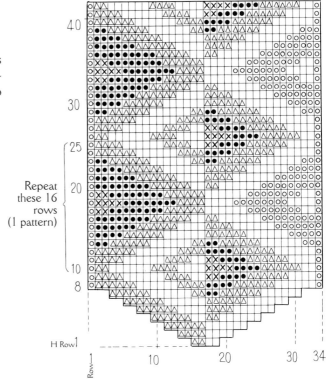

BEADS

			BAG	BELT
□	=	Rhodium	60g	50g
✕	=	Black	10g	7g
○	=	Charcoal gray	50g	25g
●	=	Matte charcoal gray	30g	25g
△	=	Matte gray	50g	40g

CHART FOR STRAP

Pattern

Solid color
(23 cm)

7

← V Row

16

← H Row 1

Repeat 7 times

CHART FOR BAG

78 Beads

○
●
◁
□
◎
●
◁
□
◎
●
◁
□
◎
← ●
← ◁
← □
← ◎
← ●
← ◁
← □
← ◎

→ Matte charcoal
→ Matte gray   (Repeat)
→ Rhodium
→ Charcoal gray

223 ⌐V Row

16

Repeat 5 times

→ 96

128

↑ 113
→ 114

85

SMALL BAG WITH RIPPLE MOTIF

Pictured on Page 8

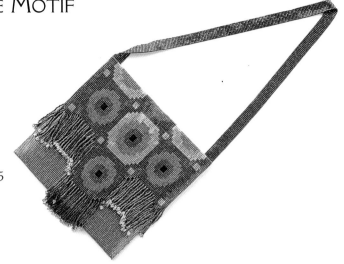

Finished measurements: 15.5 cm x 15 cm
Thread: Black
Supplies: Two pieces black fabric for 1
        lining and interfacing (20 x 40 cm
        each), black zipper (14 cm)
Warp: 90 cm x 109 threads
Vertical rows x Horizontal rows: 108 x 255
Fringe: Straight fringe (see Page 44)

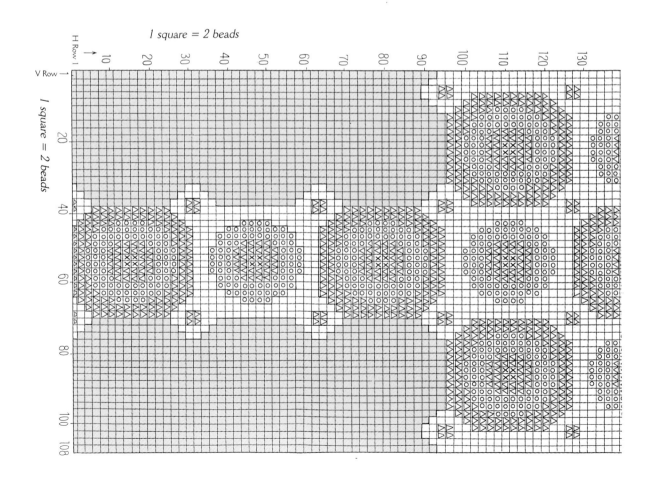

BACK

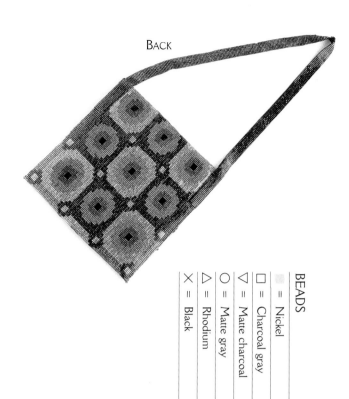

● INSTRUCTIONS

Weave Rows 1-255, hide threads, and join sides. Attach fringe to flap. Attach lining and zipper (see Pages 60-63). For the strap, warp the loom with 90 cm of double thread, and weave 350 rows of 8 beads, using charcoal gray beads. Attach 25 rows of the strap to each side of bag.

BEADS

	= Nickel	40g
□	= Charcoal gray	70g
▽	= Matte charcoal	10g
○	= Matte gray	30g
△	= Rhodium	15g
✕	= Black	5g

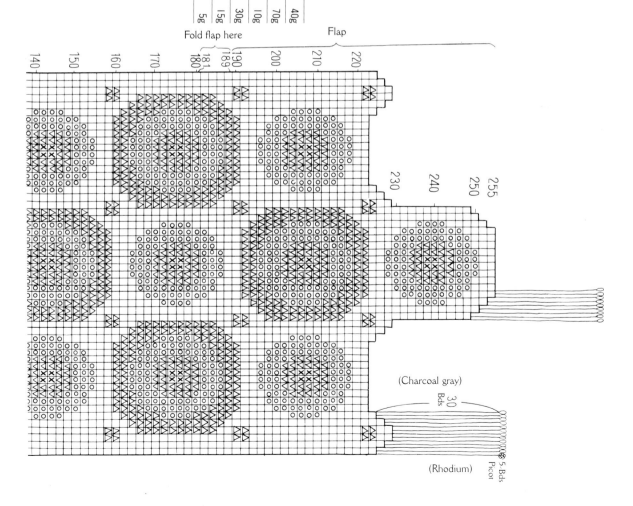

ACCESSORIES WITH FLOWER MOTIFS

Pictured on Page 11

BROOCH

Finished measurements:
  3 cm x 11 cm
Thread: Black
Supplies: Pin back (3 cm wide)
Warp: 22 threads
Vertical rows x Horizontal rows:
  21 x 41
Fringe: Twisted fringe
  (see Page 44)

● INSTRUCTIONS

Weave Rows 1-7, making increases at left and right. Hide threads. Attach fringe using separate thread (see Page 44). Attach brooch to pin back (see Page 48).

PENDANT

Finished measurements:
  2.2 cm x 49 cm
Thread: Black
Supplies: Pin back (3 cm wide)
Warp: 80 cm x 16 threads
Vertical rows x Horizontal rows:
  15 x 270
Fringe: Twisted fringe
  (see Page 44)

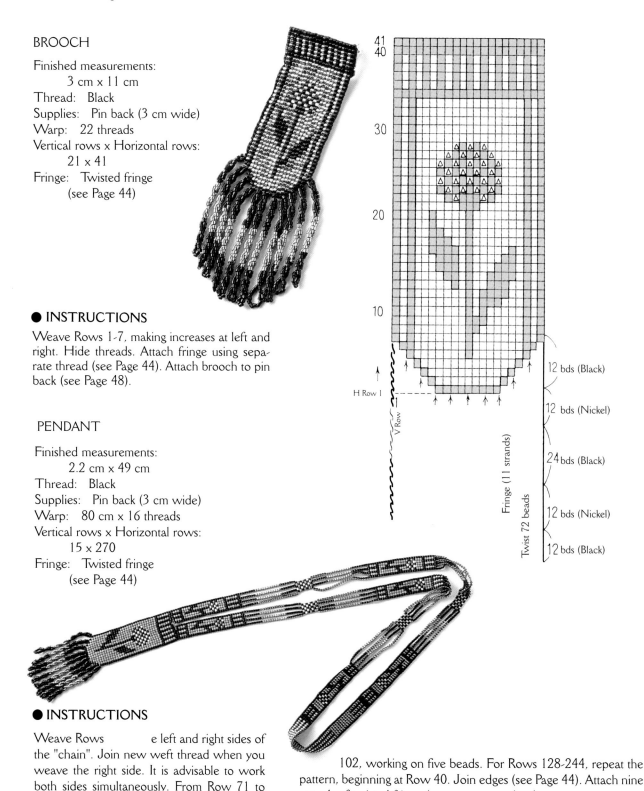

● INSTRUCTIONS

Weave Rows   e left and right sides of the "chain". Join new weft thread when you weave the right side. It is advisable to work both sides simultaneously. From Row 71 to Row 95, form the slits. Use double warp thread at both edges between Rows 96 and

102, working on five beads. For Rows 128-244, repeat the pattern, beginning at Row 40. Join edges (see Page 44). Attach nine strands of twisted fringe (see arrows on chart).

BEADS (BROOCH)

□	= Nickel	5g
▨	= Black	6g
△	= Lt rhodium (cut)	1g

BEADS (PENDANT)

□	= Nickel	10g
▨	= Black	15g
△	= Lt rhodium (cut)	3g

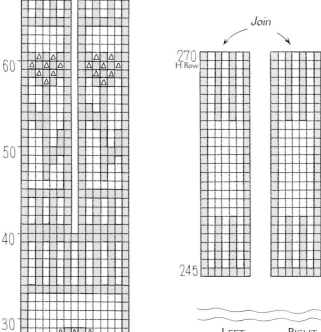

Join

270
H Row

245

LEFT   RIGHT

127

120

110

Slit

100

90

Slit   Slit   Slit   Slit   Slit   Slit

80

71

Use double warp
thread at edges only

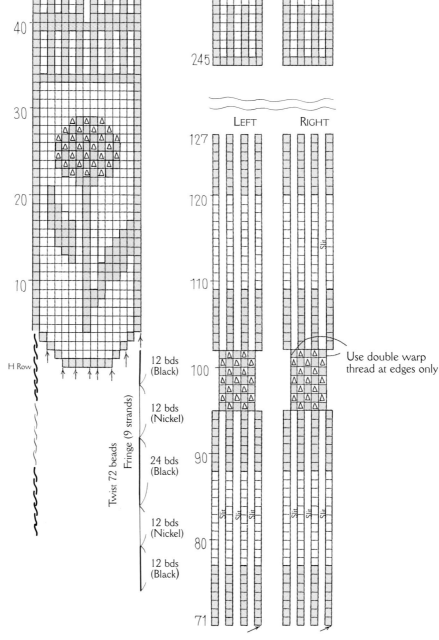

70

60

50

40

30

20

10

H Row

Twist 72 beads   Fringe (9 strands)

12 bds
(Black)

12 bds
(Nickel)

24 bds
(Black)

12 bds
(Nickel)

12 bds
(Black)

EARRINGS

Finished measurements: 1.5 cm (diameter)
Thread: Black
Supplies: Perforated earring backs
   (see Page 57).
Warp: 60 cm x 12 threads
Vertical rows x Horizontal rows: 11 x 76
   (woven piece will measure 1.5 cm x
   7.8 cm)

● INSTRUCTIONS

Weave the earrings and hide threads. Twist woven piece, and then twist it again, firmly, in the opposite direction to form a spiral. Sew ends together. Attach earring backs.

MAKING THE EARRINGS

Twist woven piece

⇩

Wind as shown

(BACK)   *Sew on earring back*

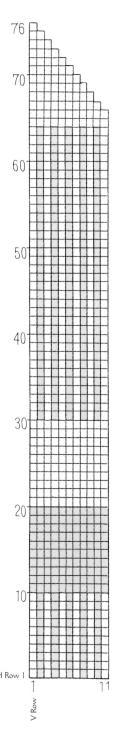

H Row 1
1   11

V Row

BEADS

□	= Nickel	5g
▨	= Black	5g

CREATING A "STITCH" CHART

You might want to try making a "stitch" chart based on the information in the chart at left. Starting with the first row, from the left, write down the number of beads for each color, using a different symbol for each. In the chart below, the "I" represents nickel, and "Ix", black. Since you will begin decreasing on the right at Row 67, you can represent the number of beads to be decreased by writing a number within a circle.

STITCH CHART

1 \ 10	I	Ix	I	Ix	I	Ix	I	Ix	i	Ix	I	
11 \ 20	I Ix											
21 \ 30	I I											
31 \ 64	I	Ix	I	Ix	I	Ix	I	Ix	I	Ix	I	
65	I I											
66	I I											
67	10	①										
68	9	②										
69	8	③										
70	7	④										
71	6	⑤										
72	5	⑥										
73	4	⑦										
74	3	⑧										
75	2	⑨										
76	1	⑩										

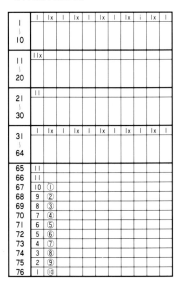

BRACELET

Finished measurements: 1 cm x 17.5 cm
Thread: Black
Supplies: Bracelet clasp
Warp: 60 cm x 8 threads
Vertical rows x Horizontal rows: 7 x 106

● INSTRUCTIONS

Weave Rows 1-31, forming slits where indicated. Repeat Rows 7-31 twice, then weave from Row 25 back to Row 1. Attach bracelet clasp (see Page 51).

BEADS

□	= Nickel	3g
■	= Black	5g
▽	= Rhodium	1g

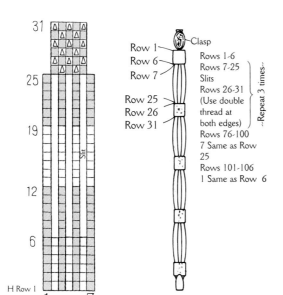

Row 1
Row 6
Row 7
Row 25
Row 26
Row 31

Clasp
Rows 1-6
Rows 7-25 Slits
Rows 26-31 (Use double thread at both edges)
Rows 76-100 7 Same as Row 25
Rows 101-106 1 Same as Row 6
~Repeat 3 times~

31
25
19
12
6
H Row 1
Slit
1   7
V Row

Finished measurements: 21.5 cm x 13.5 cm
Thread: Gray
Supplies: Two pieces of white fabric for lining and interfacing (30 x 50 cm each), silver purse frame (17 cm x 4.5 cm)
Warp: 90 cm x 146 threads
Vertical rows x Horizontal rows: 145 x 161

● INSTRUCTIONS

Weave back of purse with nickel beads only from Rows 1-80. Weave the pattern into Rows 81-161 for the front of the purse. Remove from loom. Pull the warp threads from the darts and shape bottom of purse (see Page 65). Hide threads and join sides. Attach purse frame (see Page 76). Weave the back (Rows 1-80) with nickel beads only. Weave the pattern into front of back (Rows 81-161).

SEE PAGE 92 FOR CHART

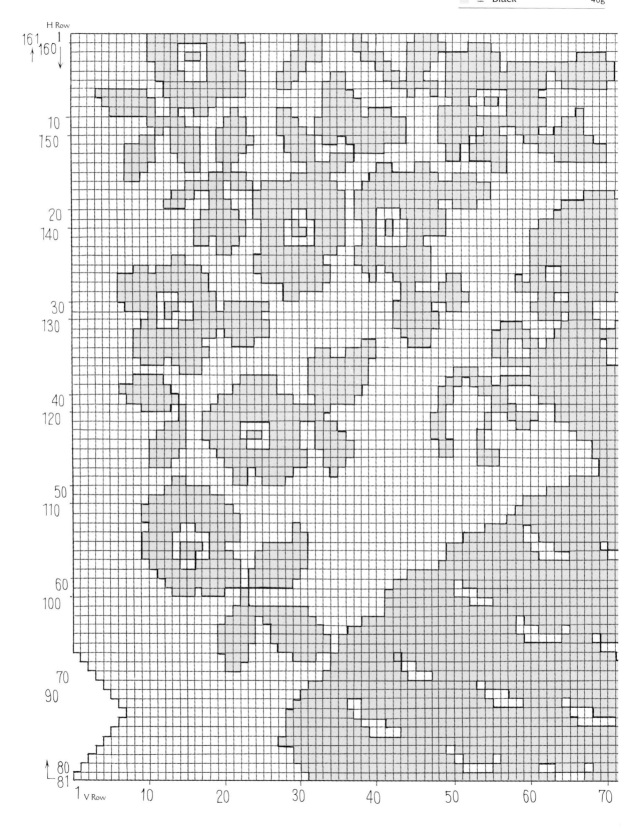

BEADS

☐ = Nickel		90g
▦ ≡ Black		40g

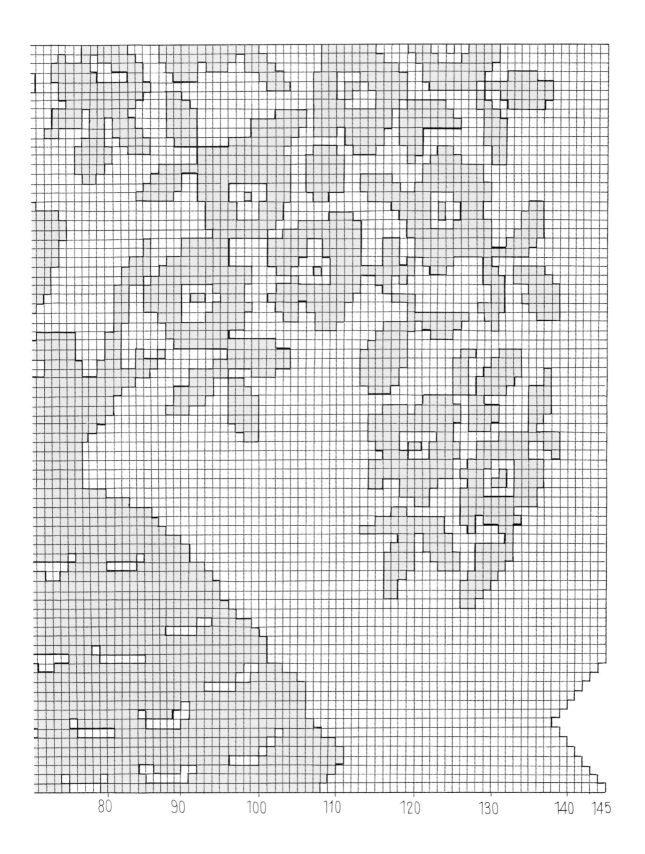

Hat Brooch

Pictured on Page 16

Finished measurements: 7 cm x 4.5 cm
Thread: Gray
Supplies: Perforated pin back
Warp: 27 threads
Vertical rows x Horizontal rows:
        26 x 110

● INSTRUCTIONS

Repeat Rows 1-55 twice. Pull warp threads to shape the hat. Hide threads. Join sides of woven piece. Make two strands of fringe, using black beads, for the ribbon. Use double thread when you attach pin back.

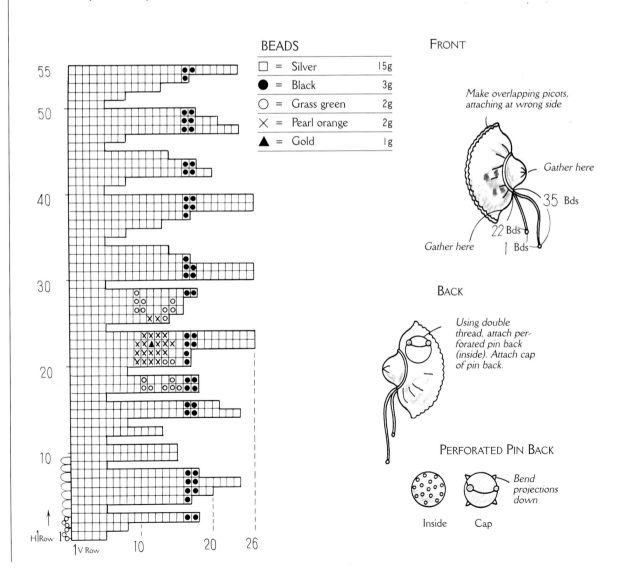

BEADS

□	=	Silver	15g
●	=	Black	3g
○	=	Grass green	2g
✕	=	Pearl orange	2g
▲	=	Gold	1g

FRONT

*Make overlapping picots,
attaching at wrong side*

Gather here

35 Bds

22 Bds

1 Bds

Gather here

BACK

*Using double
thread, attach per-
forated pin back
(inside). Attach cap
of pin back.*

PERFORATED PIN BACK

Bend
projections
down

Inside   Cap

PARASOL BROOCH

Pictured on Page 16

Finished measurements: 4.5 cm x 12 cm
Thread: Gray
Supplies: Perforated pin back, three lengths
of 28-gauge wire (30-cm each)
Warp: 48 threads, 8 threads
Vertical rows x Horizontal rows:
47 x 68 (parasol)
7 x 75 (handle)

● INSTRUCTIONS

Weave Rows 1-34; repeat. To shape parasol, pull warp threads where decreases were made; sew sides together. After you have woven the handle, insert three pieces of wire through the two beads at the center of the first row, and fold piece in half (15 cm). Apply carpenter's glue and join sides. Use pliers to cut off the excess wire at the bottom of the handle. Insert handle into parasol and attach. Attach pin back.

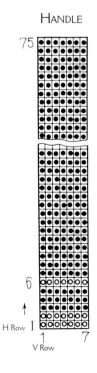

Attach perforated pin back to parasol, using double thread

Gather here

BEADS

□	=	Silver	20g
●	=	Black	5g
○	=	Grass green	2g
×	=	Pearl orange	2g
▲	=	Gold	1g

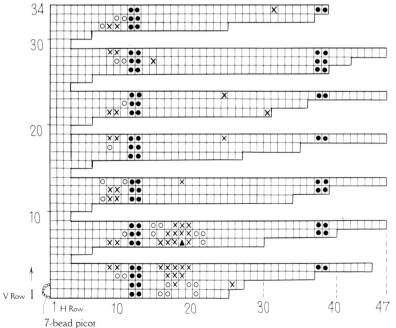

7-bead picot

HANDLE

95

BAG WITH WILD ROSES

Pictured on Page 16

Finished measurements: 14 cm x 13 cm
Thread: Gray
Supplies: White fabric for lining (22 x 35
        cm), elastic (30 cm)
Warp: 90 cm x 124 threads
Vertical rows x Horizontal rows: 123 x 216

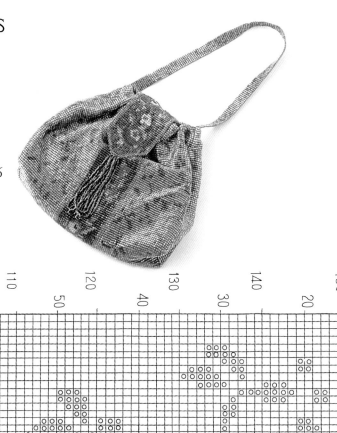

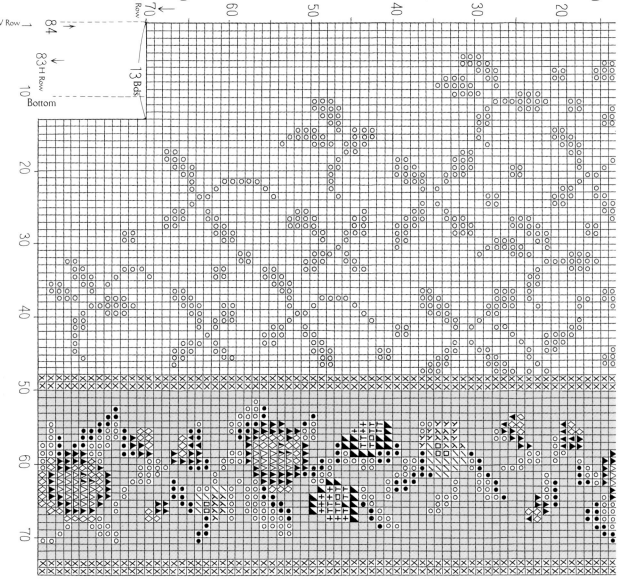

● INSTRUCTIONS

Weave up to Row 164, making decreases at left and right for the darts. For Rows 83-164, reverse the pattern, weaving back from Rows 82 through 1. At Row 165, decrease, leaving 27 beads at the center for the flap. Hide the threads, shape darts, and join sides (see Page 72). Attach 6 decorative loops to the end of the flap. Sew the lining, and insert elastic. Weave strap on 7 beads, for 300 rows. Join 20 rows to each side of bag.

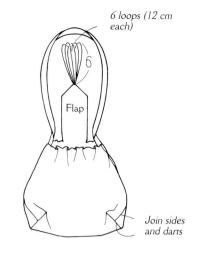

6 loops (12 cm each)

Flap

Join sides and darts

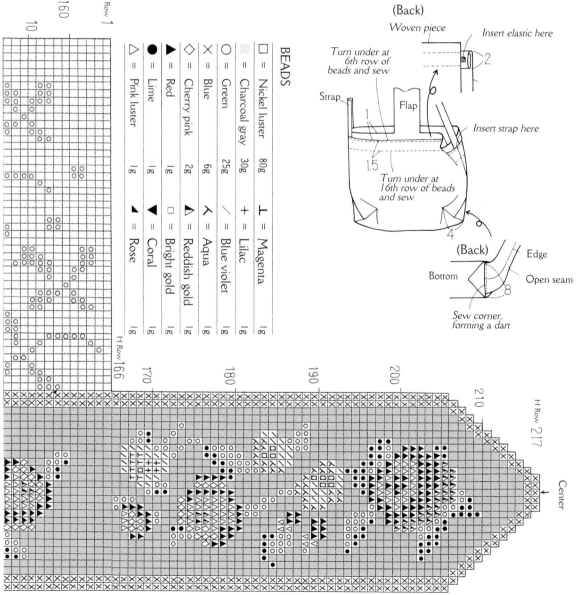

BEADS

□ = Nickel luster	80g	⊥ = Magenta	1g
▨ = Charcoal gray	30g	+ = Lilac	1g
○ = Green	25g	/ = Blue violet	1g
✕ = Blue	6g	⅄ = Aqua	1g
◇ = Cherry pink	2g	▷ = Reddish gold	1g
▶ = Red	1g	□ = Bright gold	1g
● = Lime	1g	◀ = Coral	1g
△ = Pink luster	1g	▲ = Rose	1g

(Back)

Woven piece

Insert elastic here

Turn under at 6th row of beads and sew

Strap

Flap

Insert strap here

Turn under at 16th row of beads and sew

(Back)

Edge

Bottom

Open seam

Sew corner, forming a dart

LIPSTICK HOLDER AND BELT WITH ROSES

Pictured on Page 19

LIPSTICK HOLDER

Finished measurements: 6 cm x 8.5 cm
Thread: Black
Supplies: White fabric for lining (8 x 12 cm)
Warp: 80 cm x 39 threads
Vertical rows x Horizontal rows: 38 x 156

BELT

Finished measurements: 6 cm x (waist
    measurement + 20 cm)
Thread: Black
Supplies: Belt buckle (6 cm wide)
Warp: (Length + 30 cm) x 84 threads
*(Warp with double thread except for the three
places where triple thread is indicated.)*
Vertical rows x Horizontal rows: 38 x (waist
    measurement + 20 cm)

● INSTRUCTIONS

Weave lipstick holder, hide threads, and join Rows 1
and 113. Turn woven piece under at 2nd row of
beads, and attach lining.

● INSTRUCTIONS

Begin weaving with the pattern (Rows 1-24).
Alternate pattern with 33 rows of solid matte
black. Hide threads and attach buckle (see
Page 42).

CHART FOR LIPSTICK HOLDER

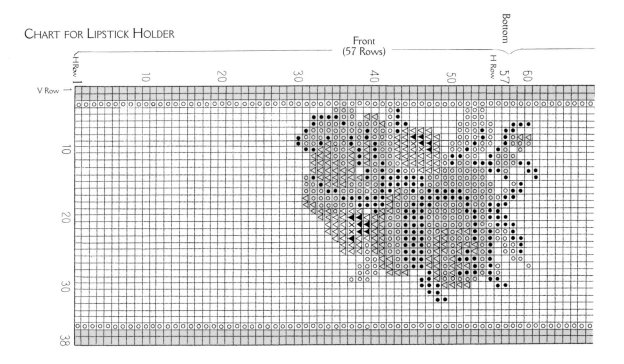

LINING FOR LIPSTICK

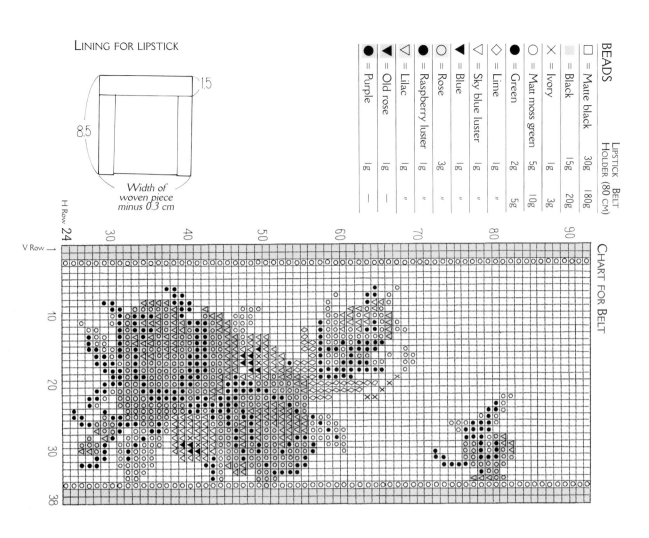

BEADS

		LIPSTICK HOLDER	BELT (80 CM)	
□	= Matte black	30g	180g	—
	= Black	15g	20g	—
✕	= Ivory	1g	3g	—
○	= Matt moss green	5g	10g	—
●	= Green	2g	5g	—
◇	= Lime	1g	1g	"
▽	= Sky blue luster	1g	1g	"
▼	= Blue	1g	1g	"
○	= Rose	3g	1g	"
●	= Raspberry luster	1g	1g	"
▽	= Lilac	1g	—	—
◀	= Old rose	1g	1g	—
●	= Purple	1g	—	—

CHART FOR BELT

CHART FOR LIPSTICK HOLDER

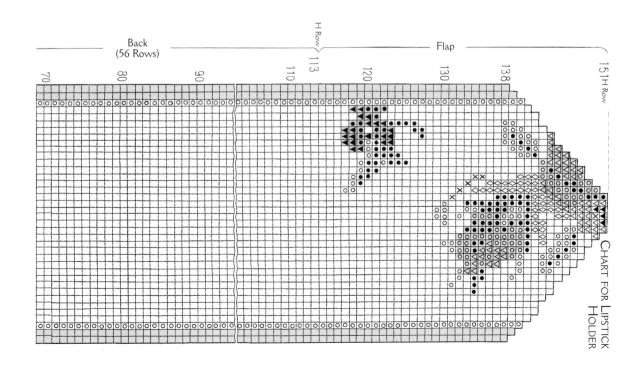

Bag With Roses

Pictured on Page 19

Finished measurements:
11.5 cm x 21 cm

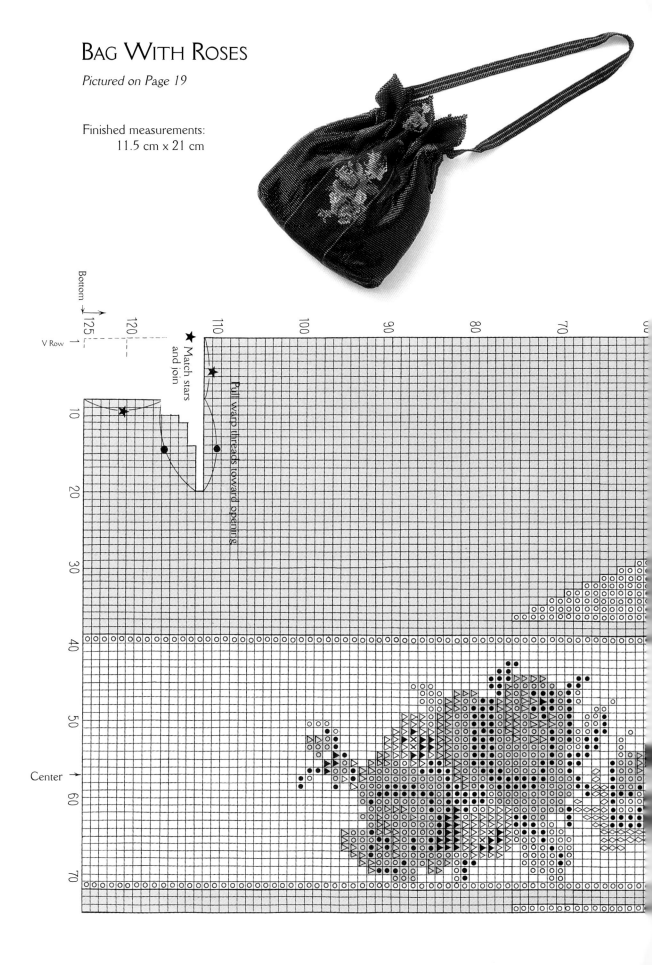

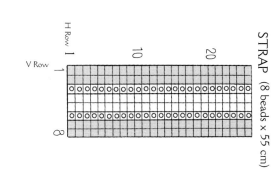

STRAP (8 beads × 55 cm)

H Row 1

10

20

V Row 1

8

BEADS

□	= Matte black	80g
▦	= Black	60g
✕	= Ivory	1g
○	= Matte moss green	20g
●	= Green	10g
◇	= Lime	3g
△	= Sky blue luster	2g
▶	= Blue	1g
○	= Rose	7g
●	= Raspberry luster	2g
△	= Lilac	3g
▶	= Old Rose	2g

50

40

30

20

10

1 H Row

101

Thread: Black
Supplies: Two pieces of fabric for lining and
interfacing (20 x 35 cm each), elastic
cord (25 cm)
Warp: 90 cm x 112 threads
120 cm x 18 threads for strap
(warp with double thread)
Vertical rows x Horizontal rows: 111 x 250

● INSTRUCTIONS

Weave from Row 1 on chart to Row 125,
and then back to Row 1. Weave the triangles
in Rows 1-26 with separate weft thread.
Weave the last two triangles at right with separate weft thread as well. Weave the strap
(56 cm). Join 23 rows of strap to each side of
the bag. Sew the lining, insert into bag and
attach. Insert elastic cord.

● SHAPING THE BOTTOM OF THE BAG

Weave Rows 1-111. Decrease in Rows 112-
125 to form the darts on the bottom. Then
weave back from Rows 125 to 1. On the bottom (Row 111), pull the warp threads from
the 9th through 20th beads toward the opening of the bag. Pull the warp threads from
Rows 111-140 toward the bottom of bag. Cut
threads at the center. Hide threads. Join bottom and darts (see Page 73).

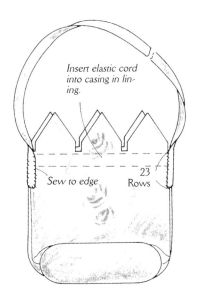

Insert elastic cord
into casing in lin-
ing.

Sew to edge   23
              Rows

GOLD BAG WITH ROSES

Pictured on Page 25

Finished measurement: 17 cm x 19 cm
Tools: Loom, needle, sewing needle
Thread: Gray
Supplies: White fabric for lining
(25 x 60 cm), gold purse frame
(13 cm x 5 cm), gold chain (100 cm))
Warp: 90 cm x 112 threads
120 cm x 18 threads for strap
(warp with double thread)
Vertical rows x Horizontal rows: 116 x 229
Fringe: Twisted fringe (see Page 44)

● INSTRUCTIONS

Weave pattern into both sides. Join sides.
Attach purse frame, lining, and chain (see
Pages 76-80).

See Page 104 for chart

Gold Corsage

Pictured on Page 25

Finished measurement: 6 cm (diameter) x c. 4 cm
Thread: Gray
Beads: Bright gold (26 g), rhodium (3 g)
Supplies: Perforated pin back
Warp: A: 20 threads
       B: 21 threads
Vertical rows x Horizontal rows:
       A: 19 x 90
       B: 20 x 126

● INSTRUCTIONS

Weave both A and B with bright gold beads. As you weave, make 2-bead picots on the left side with rhodium beads (see Page 46). Make increase and decreases on the right side to form the darts. Remove from loom and pull warp threads to shape darts. Join ends of both A and B to form a circle. Form the center of the flower with B. Attach A to B. Using double thread, attach corsage to pin back.

"Stitch" charts

A

1	19	
2	17	②
3	14	⑤
4	8	⑪
5	12	⑦
6	16	③

Repeat Rows 1-6
15 times

B

1	20	
2	20	
3	18	②
4	16	④
5	14	⑥
6	16	④
7	18	②

Repeat Rows 1-7
15 times

B

Form a circle

Gather at bottom

⇨

Insert B into A and attach. Attach pin back.

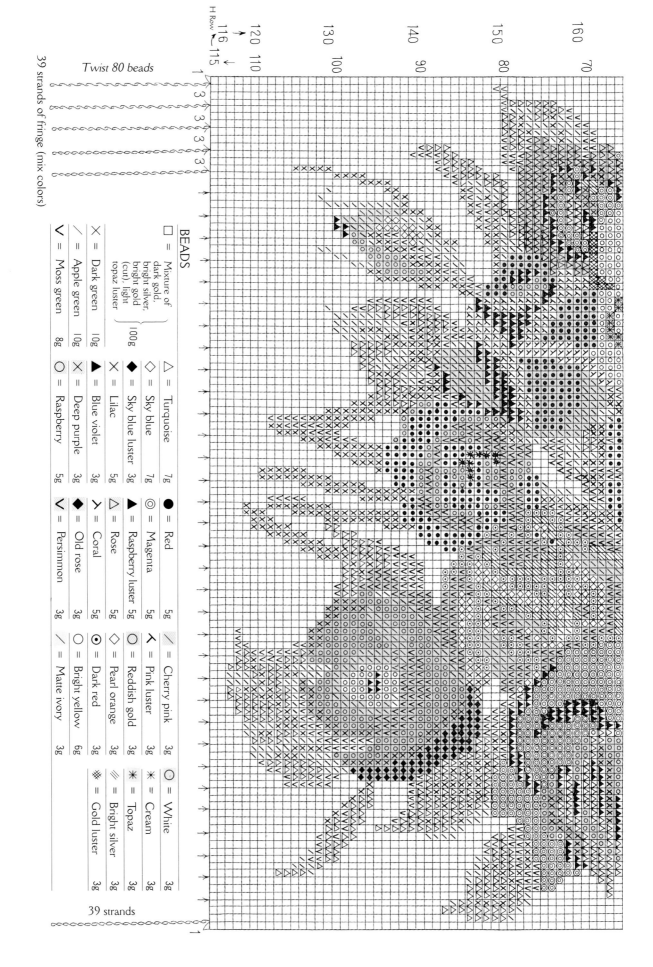

BEADS

□	=	Mixture of dark gold, bright silver, bright gold (cut), light topaz luster	100g
△	=	Turquoise	7g
◇	=	Sky blue	7g
◆	=	Sky blue luster	3g
✕	=	Lilac	5g
╱	=	Apple green	10g
✕	=	Dark green	10g
✕	=	Deep purple	3g
▲	=	Blue violet	3g
∨	=	Moss green	8g
○	=	Raspberry	5g
●	=	Red	5g
◎	=	Magenta	5g
▲	=	Raspberry luster	5g
✕	=	Rose	5g
⟋	=	Coral	5g
◉	=	Dark red	3g
◇	=	Pearl luster	3g
○	=	Reddish gold	3g
⅄	=	Pink luster	3g
╱	=	Cherry pink	3g
○	=	White	3g
○	=	Bright yellow	6g
◆	=	Old rose	3g
∨	=	Persimmon	3g
╱	=	Matte ivory	3g
○	=	Cream	3g
✳	=	Topaz	3g
⧄	=	Bright silver	3g
⧓	=	Gold luster	3g

Twist 80 beads

39 strands of fringe (mix colors)

39 strands

Chart for Gold Bag With Roses

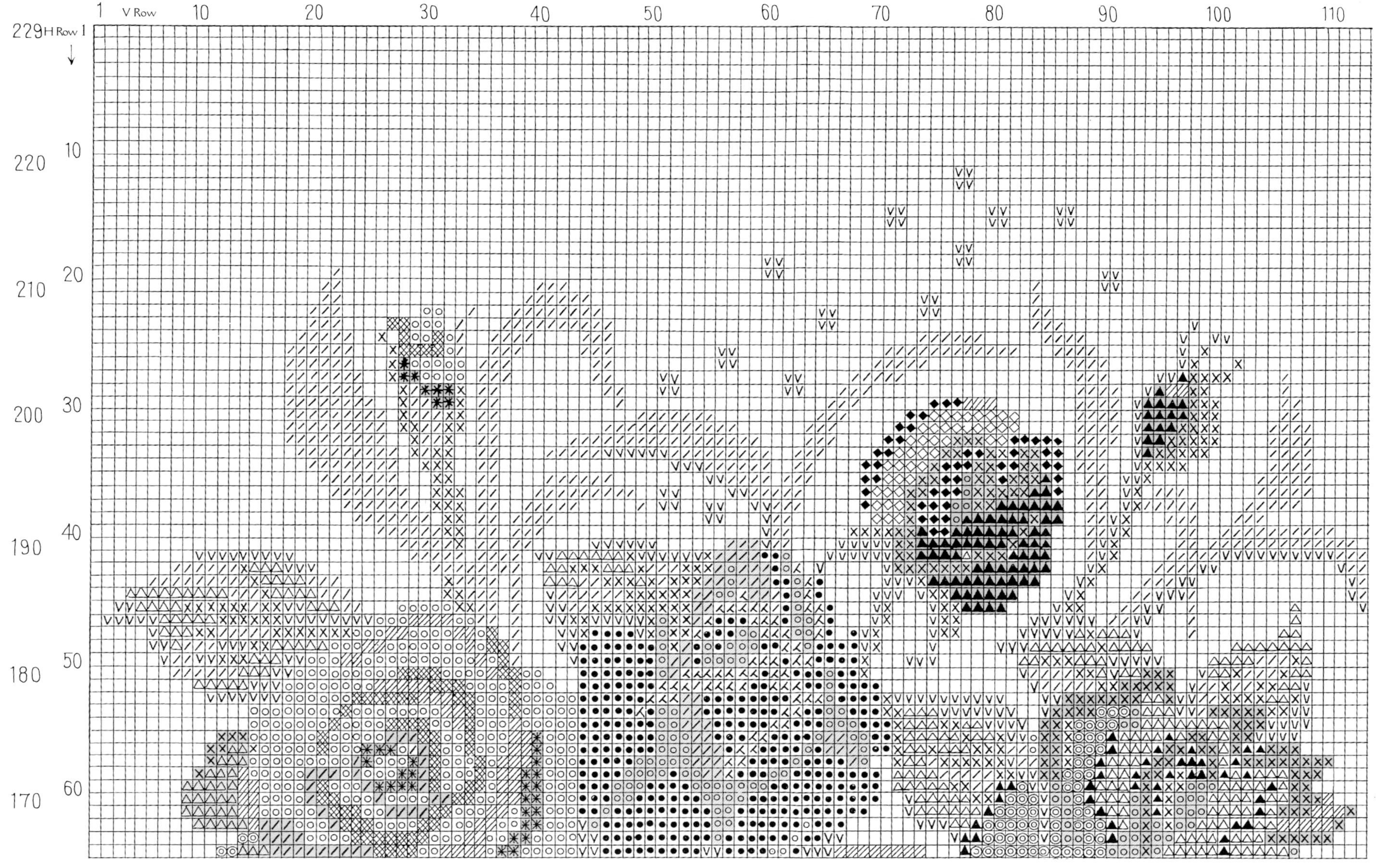

PURSE WITH ROSES

Pictured on Page 20

Finished measurement: 20 cm x 20 cm
Thread: Gray
Supplies: Green fabric for lining (25 x 60 cm), elastic (50 cm)
Warp: A: 90 cm x 126 threads
       B: 80 cm x 42 threads
       180 cm x 18 threads for strap
              (warp with double thread)
Vertical rows x Horizontal rows:
       A: 125 x 234
       B: 41 x 231
Fringe: Straight fringe (see Page 44)

● INSTRUCTIONS

For A, repeat Rows 1-77 three times. For B, repeat Rows 1-6. Pull warp threads on A and B, and join sides (see Page 42). Turn down 10 beads on the right side of A, and join to B. For the strap, work 720 rows on 8 beads (matte grass green). Attach pompom, strap, and lining (see Pages 68-71).

BEADS

Symbol	Bead	Amount
□	Bright silver	60g
(matte)	Matte grass green	80g
▶	Green	20g
/	Brown iris	20g
<	Lime	10g
\	Grass green	10g
X	Blue Gray	10g
○	Pearl orange	10g
(shaded)	Old rose	8g
△	Coral	5g
△	Red	5g
◇	Apple green	1g
(shaded)	Blue violet	1g
⊙	Aqua	1g
<	Peach	2g
●	Raspberry luster	8g
◆	Metallic bronze	2g
○	Cherry pink	5g
●	Reddish gold	8g

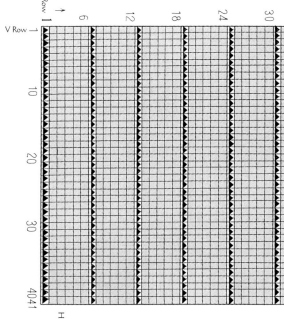

POMPOM

FRINGE

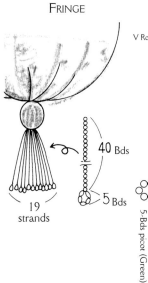

40 Bds
5 Bds
19 strands

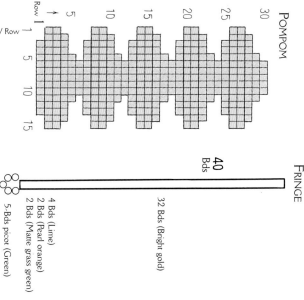

FRINGE
40 Bds
32 Bds (Bright gold)
4 Bds (Lime)
2 Bds (Pearl orange)
2 Bds (Matte grass green)
5-Bds picot (Green)

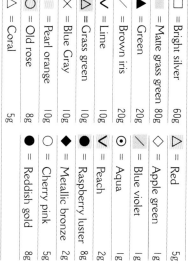

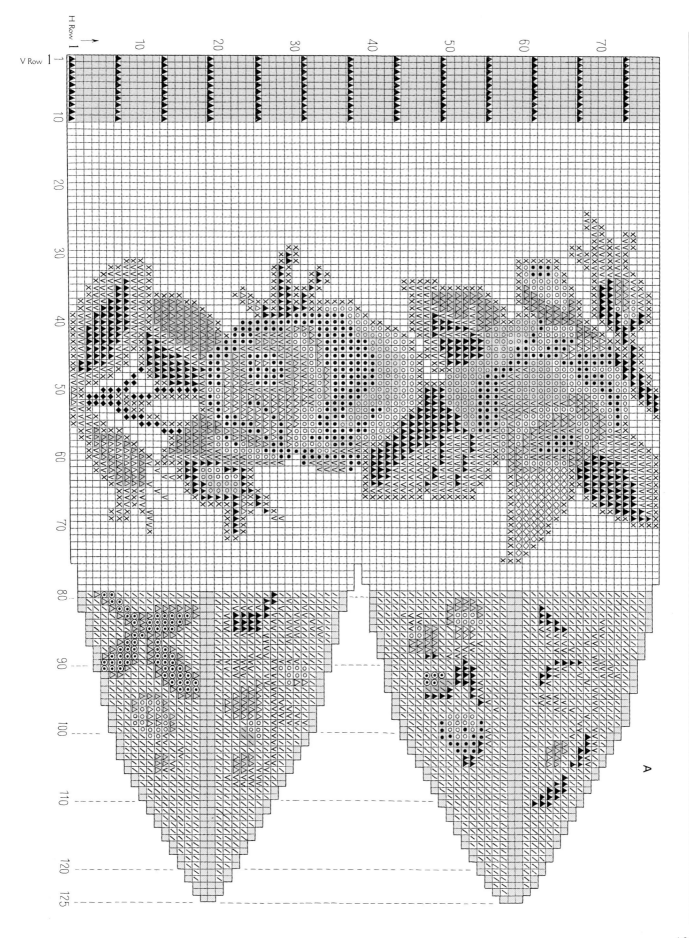

TWO BROOCHES WITH EGYPTIAN MOTIFS

Pictured on Page 29

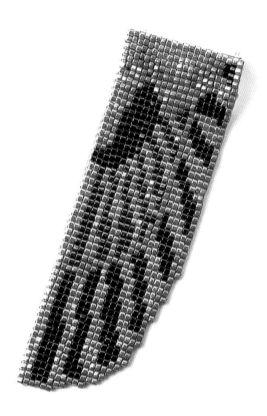

BEADS

☐	=	Dark gold	3g
▨	=	Navy blue	2g
✕	=	Pearl orange	2g
●	=	Green	2g
△	=	Bright gold	1g
╱	=	Nickel luster	1g

Finished measurement: 3 cm x 9 cm
Tools: Loom, needle, carpenter's glue
Thread: Gray
Supplies: Pin back (3 cm)
Warp: 22 threads
Vertical rows x Horizontal rows: 21 x 53

● INSTRUCTIONS

Weave 53 rows, making increases at the right side. Pull and hide warp threads. Attach pin back (see Page 49).

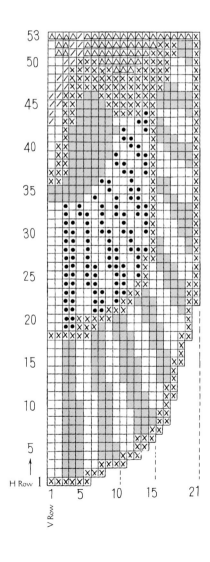

Finished measurement: 5.2 cm x 6.5 cm
Tools: Loom, needle, carpenter's glue
Thread: Gray
Supplies: Pin back (4.5 cm)
Warp: A: 38 threads
B: 12 threads
Vertical rows x Horizontal rows:
A: 37 x 22
B: 11 x 8
Fringe: Straight fringe (see Page 44)

● INSTRUCTIONS

Weave A, making increases and decreases so that no thread is visible at the edges. Starting with Row 14, leave a 1-bead opening at the center, and continue weaving to the left and right of opening. Use a new weft thread when you weave the right side. Weave B, again making increases and decreases so that no thread is visible at the edges. Starting with Row 5, weave 3 rows each on the left and right sides. Join A and B at the "x" marks shown in the charts below. Attach 16 strands of fringe to the beads marked with arrows in the charts. Attach pin back (see Page 49).

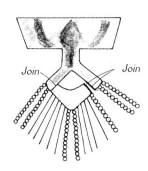

BEADS

△	= Bright gold	3g
	= Navy blue	1g
●	= Green	1g
□	= Nickel	1g

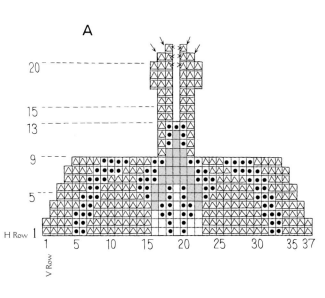

A

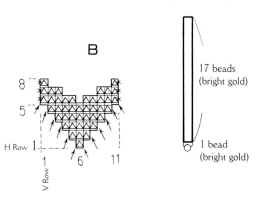

FRINGE (16 STRANDS)

17 beads
(bright gold)

1 bead
(bright gold)

B

Bag With Asian Motifs

Pictured on Page 30

Finished measurement: 17 cm x 20 cm
Thread: Gray
Supplies: White fabric for lining (25 x 60 cm),
        silver purse frame (13 x 5.5 cm),
        silver chain (100 cm)
Warp: 90 cm x 120 threads
Vertical rows x Horizontal rows: 119 x 241
Fringe: Straight fringe (see Page 44)

● INSTRUCTIONS

Weave the pattern into both back and front of the bag. Hide threads, join sides, and attach straight fringe. Attach hardware. Make and attach lining (see Pages 76-80). Attach chain.

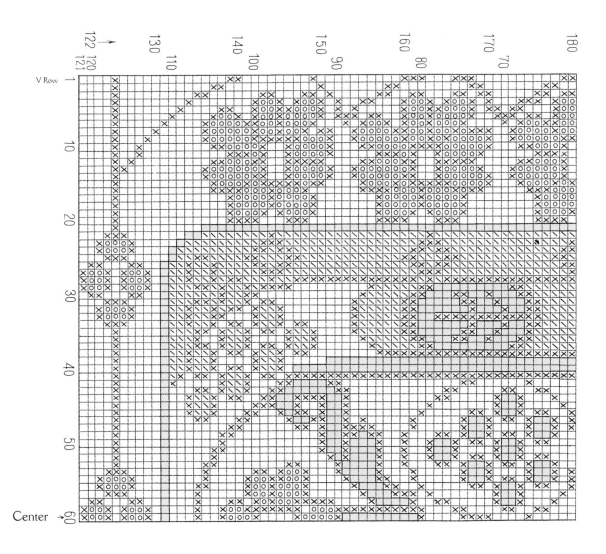

ATTACHING THE FRINGE

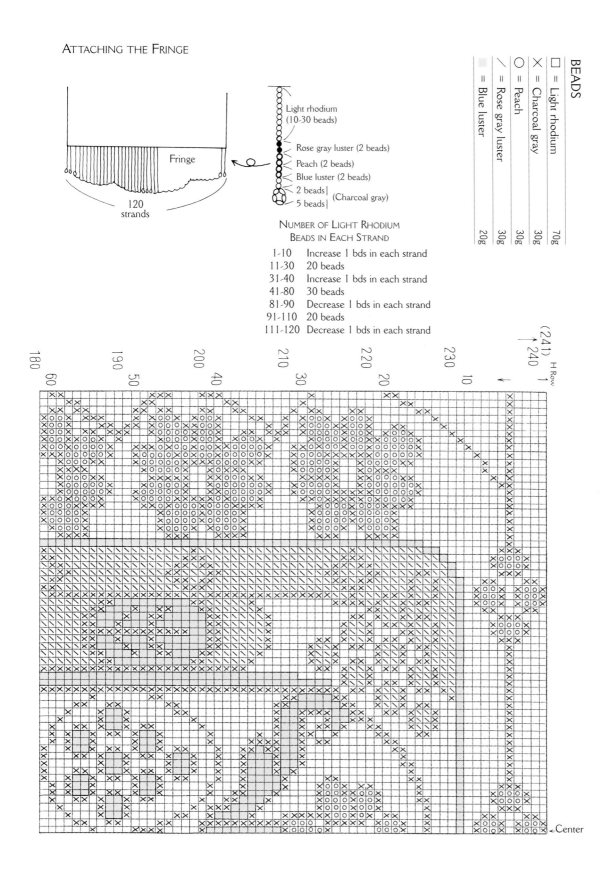

Light rhodium
(10-30 beads)

Rose gray luster (2 beads)
Peach (2 beads)
Blue luster (2 beads)
2 beads|
5 beads| (Charcoal gray)

Fringe

120 strands

NUMBER OF LIGHT RHODIUM
BEADS IN EACH STRAND

1-10	Increase 1 bds in each strand
11-30	20 beads
31-40	Increase 1 bds in each strand
41-80	30 beads
81-90	Decrease 1 bds in each strand
91-110	20 beads
111-120	Decrease 1 bds in each strand

BEADS

□	= Light rhodium	70g
✕	= Charcoal gray	30g
○	= Peach	30g
/	= Rose gray luster	30g
▨	= Blue luster	20g

PAISLEY POCHETTE

Pictured on Page 33

Finished measurement: 13.5 cm x 14 cm
Thread: Black
Supplies: Two pieces black fabric
for lining and interfacing
(18 x 37 cm each), black
zipper (12 cm)
Warp: 90 cm x 91 threads
180 cm x 16 threads
for strap
Vertical rows x
Horizontal rows:
90 x 196

● INSTRUCTIONS

Make increases and decreases to form the curved bottom. Weave the pochette, and then the flap. Weave the pattern into the front of the pochette, and the back in solid black. Increase and decrease at the bottom so that the weft threads do not show. The flap will have a nicer appearance if you run the warp threads through about 10 cm of beads when you hide them. Attach lining and zipper. For the strap, weave 115 cm on 7 black beads; attach to pochette behind the lining.

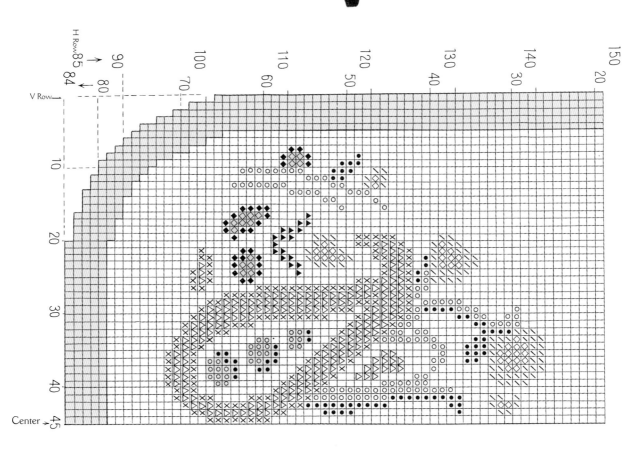

BEADS

□	= Black	90g	✕	= Bright silver	2g		
▨	= Brown luster	20g	▶	= Topaz	″		
△	= Dark gold	4g	◇	= Sky blue	″		
╱	= Pearl peach	2g	◆	= Blue	″		
◇	= Sky blue luster	″	●	= Dark red	″		
○	= Lime	″	◐	= Raspberry luster	″		
●	= Green	″					

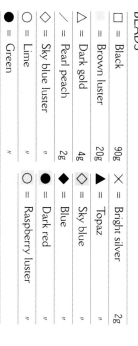

Flap

8

18 Rows

Attach strap here

Zipper

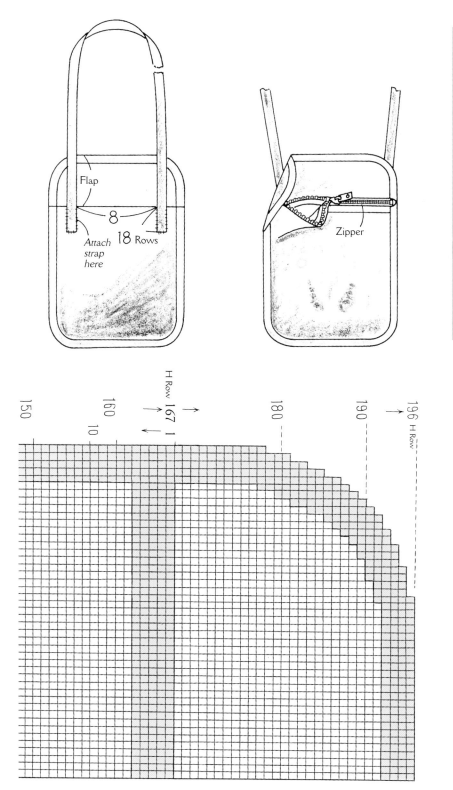

150
160
10
H Row 167 1
180
190
196 H Row
H Row

PERFUME VIAL HOLDER

Pictured on Page 33

Finished measurement: 27 cm x 10 cm
Thread: Black
Warp: 37 threads
Vertical rows x Horizontal rows:
        36 x 32
Fringe: Twisted fringe (see Page 44)

● INSTRUCTIONS

Weave Rows 1-6, forming slits as you work
(see Page 44). On Row 7, decrease so that
threads do not show, until 9 beads remain.
Continue weaving until you reach Row 32.
Join the sides of the piece, from Rows 1-6,
to form a cylinder. Attach netting to Row 7,
using 7 beads for each mesh, and working
for 10 rows (see Page 46). Gather the last
row and attach 5 strands of twisted fringe.
For the strap, use double thread 220 cm
long.   String 70 cm of black beads onto
each strand. Twist strands together.

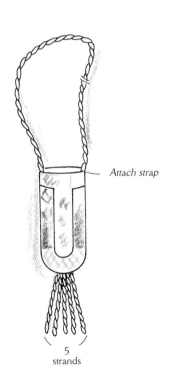

Attach strap

5
strands

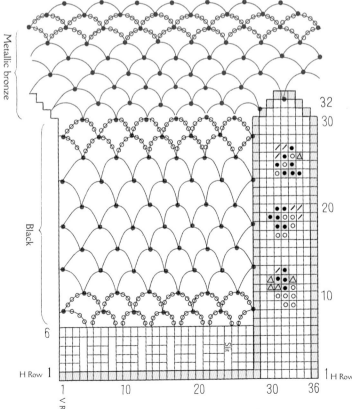

PURSE INSPIRED BY THE TSUJIGAHANA (ILLUSIONARY) DYEING STYLE

Pictured on Page 34

FRINGE

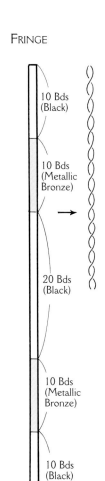

10 Bds (Black)

10 Bds (Metallic Bronze)

20 Bds (Black)

10 Bds (Metallic Bronze)

10 Bds (Black)

Finished measurement: 20.5 cm x 13.5 cm
Thread: Gray
Supplies: Two pieces of white fabric for lining and interfacing (25 x 50cm each) gold purse frame (17 x 6 cm), gold chain (38 cm)
Warp: 90 cm x 146 threads
Vertical rows x Horizontal rows: 145 x 161

● INSTRUCTIONS

Weave the pattern into both the front and back of the purse. Increase and decrease between Rows 68 and 94 for the darts at the bottom. When you have finished weaving the purse, pull the warp threads at the darts. Join sides. Attach purse frame, lining (see Pages 76-80), and chain.

BEADS

□	= Black	20g
▒	= Metallic Bronze	5g
○	= Old rose	lg
△	= Lilac	Bds
●	= Raspberry luster	"
╱	= Lime	"
●	= Green	"
●	= Bright gold (netting)	"

115

CHART FOR PURSE INSPIRED BY THE TSUJIGAHANA (ILLUSIONARY) DYEING STYLE

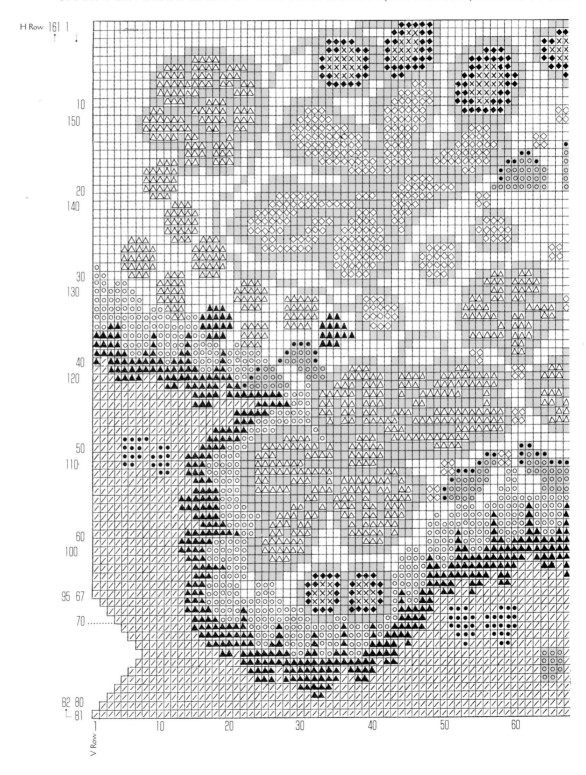

116

BEADS

□	= Deep green	50g	●	= Green	2g
▓	= Charcoal gray	25g	◇	= Sky blue luster	10g
╱	= Mixture of rose gray and light bronze iris (2:1)	25g	◆	= Blue violet	10g
△	= Dark gold	25g	✕	= Rose gray	10g
▲	= Matte Khaki	20g	●	= Dark red	3g
○	= Matte grass green	20g	◉	= Raspberry luster	3g
			V	= Pearl gray	3g

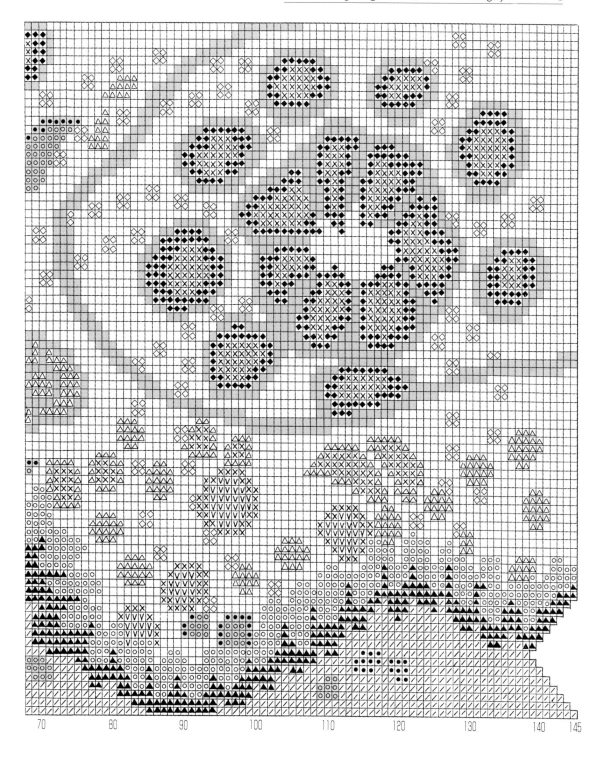

PURSE WITH JAPANESE-STYLE FLOWER PATTERN

Pictured on Page 37

Finished measurement: 16 cm x 19 cm
Thread: Beige
Supplies: White fabric for lining (20 x 50 cm),
    gold purse frame (13 x 7 cm), gold
    chain (100 cm)
Warp: 90 cm x 111 threads
Vertical rows x Horizontal rows: 110 x 221
Fringe: Netted fringe (see Page 46)

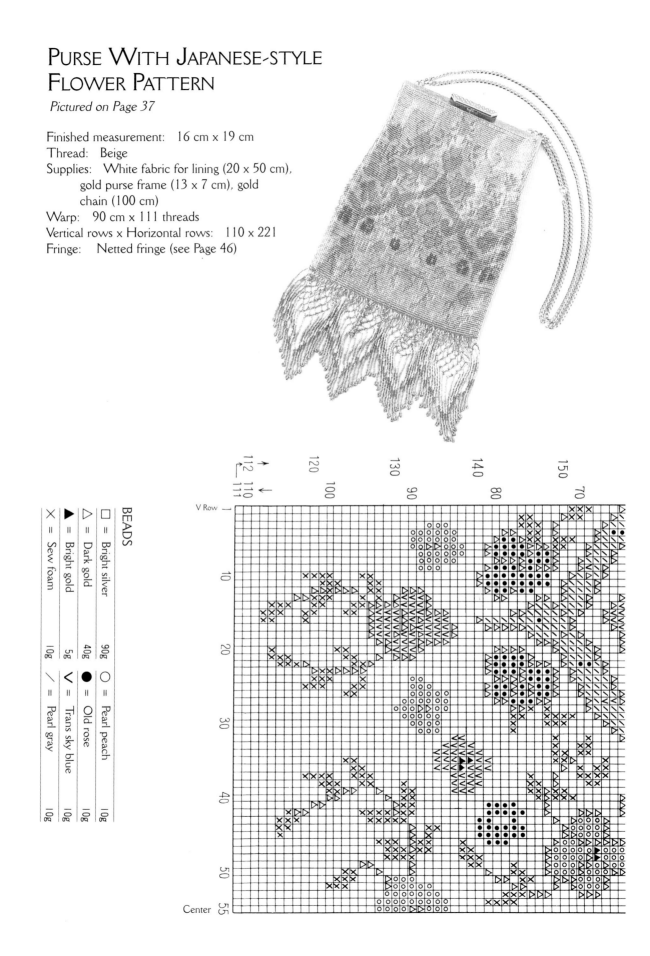

BEADS

□ =	Bright silver	90g	○ = Pearl peach	10g
△ =	Dark gold	40g	● = Old rose	10g
▶ =	Bright gold	5g	∨ = Trans sky blue	10g
✕ =	Sew foam	10g	╱ = Pearl gray	10g

● INSTRUCTIONS

Weave the purse, following the chart. Hide threads and join sides. Attach fringe to bottom. Attach purse frame, lining (see Pages 76-80), and chain.

ATTACHING THE FRINGE

4 Blocks

12 Bright silver bds

7 Dark gold bds

5 Bright silver bds

5 Old rose bds

13 Dark gold bds

5 Bright gold bds

9 Loops

Bright gold bds

Dark gold bds

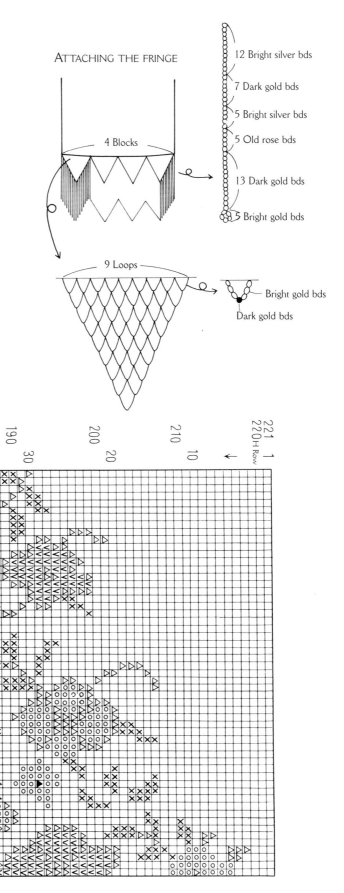

Bag With Tortoise-Shell Pattern

Pictured on Page 39

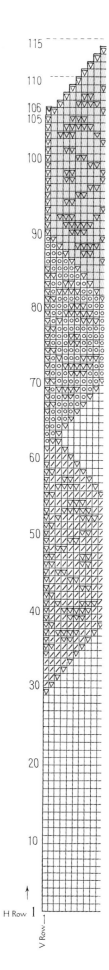

Finished measurement: 14.5 cm x 20 cm
Thread: Gray
Supplies: Two pieces white fabric for lining and
interfacing (19 x 60 cm each), gold purse
frame (12 x 6 cm), gold chain (100 cm)
Warp: 90 cm x 102 threads x 2
Vertical rows x Horizontal rows:
101 x 115 (front); 101 x 106 (back)

BEADS

□ = Reddish brown	80g
▽ = Bright gold	40g
▦ = Dark gold	20g
╱ = Rhodium	20g
○ = Pearl pink	20g

●INSTRUCTIONS

For the front of the bag, weave Rows 1-105. From
Rows 106-115, make decreases to form the triangles.
For the back, weave Rows 1-106. Hide threads. Join
the two pieces at the bottom (Row 105 of the front
and Row 106 of the back). (See Page 42). Join sides
of bag, and attach purse frame, lining (see Pages 76-
80), and chain.

Small Envelope Purse

Pictured on Page 39

Finished measurement: 19 cm x 12.5 cm
Thread: Gray
Supplies: Two pieces white fabric for lining and
interfacing (24 x 60 cm each), two lengths
of steel boning (18 cm each)
Warp: 90 cm x 128 threads
Vertical rows x Horizontal rows:
127 x 231

● INSTRUCTIONS

Begin with the flap, proceeding as shown in the diagram at lower left. Hide threads. Line up Row 81 with Row 231 and join sides. The flap will look more attractive if you run the warp threads through 15 cm of beads when you hide them. Sew lining. Insert steel boning into casing at top of bag; sew opening shut (see Page 60).

CUTTING AND SEWING THE LINING

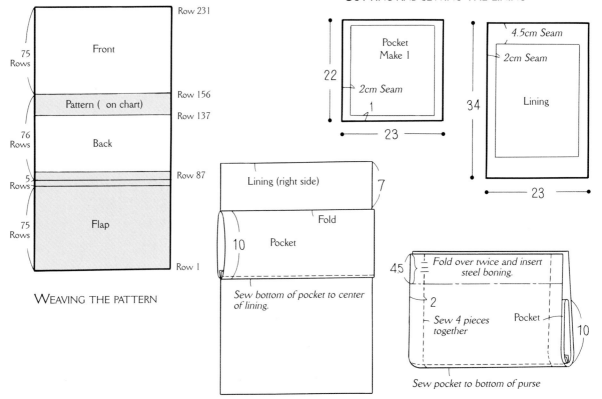

WEAVING THE PATTERN

Row 231 — Front — 75 Rows
Row 156
Pattern (on chart) — Row 137
76 Rows — Back
Row 87 — 5 Rows
75 Rows — Flap
Row 1

Pocket Make 1 — 22 — 23 — 2cm Seam — 1

4.5cm Seam — 2cm Seam — Lining — 34 — 23

Lining (right side) — 7 — Fold — 10 — Pocket
Sew bottom of pocket to center of lining.

45 — Fold over twice and insert steel boning. — 2 — Sew 4 pieces together — Pocket — 10
Sew pocket to bottom of purse

□	=	Matte nickel	90g
▦	=	Dark gold	30g
△	=	Bright gold	30g
○	=	Light rhodium	20g

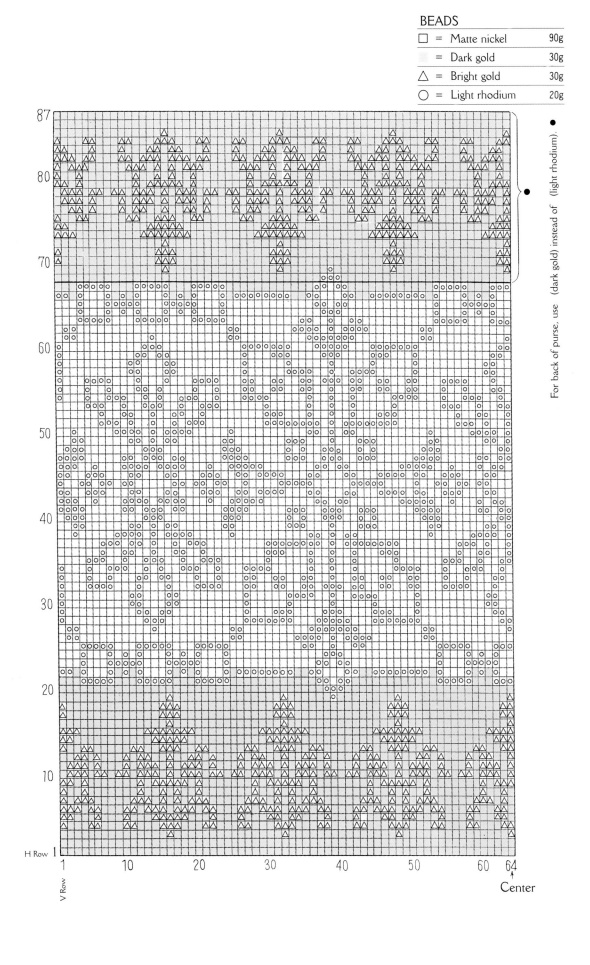

● For back of purse, use ▦ (dark gold) instead of ○ (light rhodium).

The History of Bead weaving

Bead weaving is a craft that combines color, shape, and light- the light refracted by the beads. The delicate patterns used and the metallic sheen of the beads create a sublime effect, and a harmony that evokes a mysterious warmth.

The bead woven handbags that were fashionable in Europe at the beginning of the 20th century were refined both in color and form. However, the craft traces back not to Europe, but to the native peoples of North America and the ornaments they wove from beads.

Native North Americans crafted white, black, and purple beads from clam shells. From those beads, they made decorative items that came to signify wealth and status. They also used beads for money (wampum).

In the 16th century, Europeans arrived in North America, bringing colored glass beads with them, which they gave to the Native Americans as gifts. When Jamestown was founded in Virginia in 1607, a glass factory operated by a Venetian craftsman, at which colored glass beads were manufactured, was established. Through trade with the settlers, Native Americans soon obtained large quantities of those beads. They used them in religious rites. Mothers fashioned primitive looms by winding thread around their hands and feet, and wove beads into ornaments to adorn their daughters at coming-of-age ceremonies.

Even today, Native Americans use the same techniques, totally different from those used in Europe, to make their traditional costumes, weaving bright-colored beads into geometric patterns. The necklaces they weave and sell as souvenirs are known throughout the world.

BEAD WOVEN POUCH
(Belgium, late 18th century)

PENDANT WOVEN FROM METAL BEADS
(France, c. 1920)

During the age of colonialism, woven beadwork brought back to the nations of Europe by travellers was adapted by craftsmen, and eventually gave way to techniques and designs that were completely European.

Some of the oldest examples of beadwork that demonstrate Native-American influence are open-work patterns and beautiful, intricate bead woven necklaces and bracelets produced in England in the late 18th century.

In Victorian England (mid-19th century), patterns and techniques were further refined, and the resulting, exquisite accessories became immensely popular. Elsewhere in Europe, craftspeople were incorporating regional designs into their beautiful beadwork. The high watermark was reached in the 1920's and 1930's, the Art Deco era. During this brief golden age, techniques for manufacturing and weaving beads reached their apex, and noble women carried bead woven handbags and wore jewelry woven from beads made of steel and other metals. Even today, decades later, the form and color of the articles that remain from that era, and the highly-advanced techniques employed in their making continue to fascinate.

The two world wars gave way to an age of modernism and, for a time, beadwork fell out of favor. But now it is possible, again, to enjoy bead weaving, not only in the United States but also in all parts of Europe. Through the traditional craft of bead weaving, both in the form in which it originated with native North Americans, and its Westernized form, we can take pleasure in creating beauty with our own hands.

I hope to help keep this tradition alive by drawing on my research on bead weaving and my imagination to create new designs befitting this new age.

Handbag woven from metal beads
(Germany, c. 1920)

Pendant woven by native North Americans *(purchased 1958)*

2-NEEDLE BEAD-WEAVING TECHNIQUE

Many of the rich projects and patterns presented in this book will require the use of a beading loom specifically designed for wide bead-weaving. A simple two needle weaving technique as described below will make bead weaving a joy, eliminating any pre-counting of beads while allowing you to selectively incorporate one or more beads into the work,

Two Needle Bead Weaving Technique

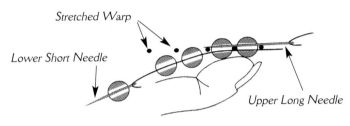

Stretched Warp

Lower Short Needle

Upper Long Needle

Loose beads for picking up by short needle

One or more loose beads are picked up by the short LOWER NEEDLE and then held between warp threads with your finger while the long UPPER NEEDLE is passed through them, holding them in place.

The two needle method uses 2 separate weft threads. Referring to illustrations, a standard length blunt pointed beading needle is used on the lower weft thread to pick up one or more beads while a long blunt pointed beading needle feeds the upper weft thread through the beads as they are placed between the warp threads.

Thus when doing a background of the same color, a large quantity of uncounted beads can be threaded and incorporated into the weaving. When you get near the design, excess beads can be dropped off and the selected color beads can be threaded in small manageable units. A blunt needle is necessary to avoid splitting the warp threads when passing though the beads. In passing the upper (long) needle, take care that one bead lies between each pair of warp threads. At the end warp threads, cross the upper and lower threads as shown.

It will be most comfortable passing the threaded weft in one direction, typically right-to-left if right-handed. To do so it will be necessary to rotate the loom, 180° after the completion of each row. For comfort, the weaving area is best kept near the middle of the loom.

In working with many colors of beads the following techniques are suggested.

For background and large areas of one color, it is suggested that you work

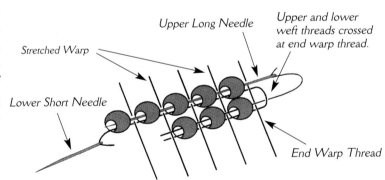

Upper Long Needle

Upper and lower weft threads crossed at end warp thread.

Stretched Warp

Lower Short Needle

End Warp Thread

SHORT NEEDLE and thread always remains under warp threads while LONG NEEDLE always remains over warp threads. Cross or wrap threads around end warp thread.

from strung beads which are typically sold in hanks with strands approximately 18" long. Beads are easily transferred from the strung put-up to your beading needle thread by simply running the needle through the beads while keeping the strand taut.

For the areas of design requiring many color changes, it is suggested that you lay lengths of double sticky tape on an index card or other stiff material and dump a small quantity of beads onto the card. Selected beads are easily picked up from this card with your threaded short needle.

Symmetrical design permits weaving from either side as required for 2-needle weaving.

Continuous warp is quickly prepared and permits rotation around frame as weaving progresses

Eccentrically mounted end frame bars permit simple tension control and warp rotation.

Board resting on lower warp threads supports design cartoon.

LACIS
BEAD LOOM

Strand of beads of same size as being woven serves as warp spacer.

Legs raise frame for ease of working and serve as warping frame for extended warps.

Bead loom

Quick release for removal of loom

Incline adjustment and lock

Rotating yoke permits weaving from both sides of loom as required for 2-needle weaving.

Adjustable for sit-down or stand-up weaving with full height adjustment.

Stand assembles and disassembles without tools and fits compactly into a 18" x 6' x 6" space.

The LACIS bead loom illustrated, is specifically designed for 2-needle wide bead weaving. Set up and warping is done in a matter of minutes and the loom is designed to be used from either end. It incorporates integral warp tension control and when used with its related floor stand it is easily rotated after the completion of each row. The active weaving area is maintained in the center of the loom by simple warp rotation as the work proceeds.

Bonded nylon thread is recommended for the warp. It is a very strong 3-ply tight twisted thread which will not untwist and is resistant to splitting. Size "B" or "C" is suggested , depending on the size of the bead. "B" for size 11 and finer and "C" for larger beads.

**BEAD LOOM MOUNTED
ON FLOOR STAND**

LACIS PUBLISHES AND DISTRIBUTES BOOKS SPECIFICALLY RELATED TO THE TEXTILE ARTS, FOCUS-ING ON THE SUBJECTS OF LACE AND LACE MAKING, COSTUME, EMBROIDERY AND HAND SEWING.

OTHER LACIS BOOKS OF INTEREST:

THE CARE AND PRESERVATION OF TEXTILES, KAREN FINCH & GRETA PUTNAM

THE ART OF HAIR WORK, MARK CAMPBELL

CROSS-STITCH ALPHABETS & TREASURES, ED. BY JULES & KAETHE KLIOT

SMOCKING & FINE SEWING, ED BY JULES & KAETHE KLIOT

MODERN DANCING (1914), MR & MRS VERNON CASTLE

MILLINERY FOR EVERY WOMAN, GEORGINA KERR KAYE

TECHNIQUE OF LADIES' HAIR DRESSING (19TH C.): CAMPBELL & MALLEMONT

KNITTING: 19TH C. SOURCES: ED. JULES & KAETHE KLIOT

HAUTE COUTURE EMBROIDERY: THE ART OF LESAGE, PALMER WHITE

THE MARY FRANCES SEWING BOOK, JANE EAYRE FRYER

THE MARY FRANCES KNITTING AND CROCHETING BOOK, JANE EAYRE FRYER

THE MARY FRANCES HOUSEKEEPER, JANE EAYRE FRYER

THE MARY FRANCES COOK BOOK, JANE EAYRE FRYER

THE MARY FRANCES GARDEN BOOK, JANE EAYRE FRYER

NETTING: FROM EARLY SOURCES, ED. JULES & KAETHE KLIOT

CROCHET: EDGINGS & INSERTIONS, ELIZA A. TAYLOR & BELLE ROBINSON

CROCHET: EDGINGS & MORE, ED. JULES & KAETHE KLIOT

CROCHET: NOVELTIES, ED. JULES & KAETHE KLIOT

CROCHET: MORE EDGINGS, ED. JULES & KAETHE KLIOT

CROCHET: DOLLS & NOVELTIES, ED. JULES & KAETHE KLIOT

THE NEEDLE MADE LACES OF RETICELLA. ED JULES & KAETHE KLIOT

CASALGUIDI STYLE LINEN EMBROIDERY, EFFIE MITROFANIS

THE ART OF SHETLAND LACE, SARAH DON

CREATING ORIGINAL HAND-KNITTED LACE, MARGARET STOVE

BERLIN WORK, SAMPLERS & EMBROIDERY OF THE 19TH C. RAFFAELLA SERENA

THE MAGIC OF FREE MACHINE EMBROIDERY, DOREEN CURRAN

DESIGNS FOR CHURCH EMBROIDERIES, THOMAS BROWN & SON

EMBROIDERY WITH BEADS, ANGELA THOMPSON

BEADED BAGS AND MORE, ED. BY JULES & KAETHE KLIOT

BEAD EMBROIDERY, JOAN EDWARDS

BEAD EMBROIDERY, VALERIE CAMPBELL-HARDING AND PAMELA WATTS

INNOVATIVE BEADED JEWELRY TECHNIQUES, GINEKE ROOT

BEADED ANIMALS IN JEWELRY, LETTY LAMMENS AND ELS SCHOLTE

CLASSIC BEADED PURSE PATTERNS, E. DE JONG-KRAMER

BEAD WEAVING: ACCESSORIES, TAKAKO SAKO

BEAD WEAVING: ELEGANCE, TAKAKO SAKO

LOCKER HOOKING, LEONE PEGUERO

TATTED LACE OF BEADS: TECHNIQUE OF BEANILE LACE, NINA LIBIN

TATTING: DESIGNS FROM VICTORIAN LACE CRAFT, ED.BY JULES & KAETHE KLIOT

THE ART OF TATTING, KATHERINE HOARE

TATTING WITH VISUAL PATTERNS, MARY KONIOR

PRACTICAL TATTING, PHYLLIS SPARKS

NEW DIMENSIONS IN TATTING, TO DE HAAN-VAN BEEK

THE DMC BOOK OF CHARTED TATTING DESIGNS, KIRSTINE & INGE NIKOLAJSEN

THE ART OF NETTING, JULES & KAETHE KLIOT

TENERIFFE LACE, JULES & KAETHE KLIOT

THE BARGELLO BOOK, FRANCES SALTER

FLORENTINE EMBROIDERY, BARBARA MULLER

FOR A COMPLETE LIST OF LACIS TITLES, WRITE TO:

LACIS
3163 ADELINE STREET
BERKELEY, CA 94703 USA